PAULIST PRESS

Review Copy

We look forward to receiving your review. Please be sure to send us two copies when it appears. Thank you.

Hugh G. Lally
PAULIST PRESS
997 Macarthur Boulevard,
Mahwah, N.J. 07430
(201) 825-7300

PASSIONATE WOMEN:
TWO MEDIEVAL MYSTICS

The Madeleva Lecture in Spirituality

This series, sponsored by the Center for Spirituality, Saint Mary's College, Notre Dame, Indiana, honors annually the woman who as president of the college inaugurated its pioneering program in theology, Sister M. Madeleva, C.S.C.

1985
Monika K. Hellwig
Christian Women in a Troubled World

1986
Sandra M. Schneiders
Women and the Word

1987
Mary Collins
Women at Prayer

1988
Maria Harris
Women and Teaching

PASSIONATE WOMEN: TWO MEDIEVAL MYSTICS

ELIZABETH DREYER

1989 Madeleva Lecture
in Spirituality

PAULIST PRESS
New York/Mahwah

Library of Congress Cataloging-in-Publication Data

Dreyer, Elizabeth, 1945–
    Passionate women : two medieval mystics / Elizabeth Dreyer.
        p.   cm.
    "1989 Madeleva lecture in spirituality."
    Bibliography: p.
    ISBN 0-8091-3082-3 : $2.95
    1. Hildegard, Saint, 1098–1179. 2. Hadewijch, 13th cent.
3. Spiritual life—Middle Ages, 600–1500. 4. Love—Religious
aspects—Christianity—History of doctrines—Middle Ages, 600–1500.
5. Mysticism—History—Middle Ages, 600–1500. 6. Women mystics—
Biography. I. Title. II. Title: Madeleva lecture in
spirituality.
BV5095.A1D7   1989
248.2'2'0922—dc19
    [B]   89-30048
                                                                              CIP

Published by Paulist Press
997 Macarthur Blvd.
Mahwah, N.J. 07430

Printed and bound in the United States of America

TABLE OF CONTENTS

To my husband,
John Bennett

INTRODUCTION

We no longer view the capacities of the human person in segregated, compartmentalized spheres. Science repeatedly discovers new inner connections and interdependencies that mandate a wholistic approach to the human person. However, even though the heyday of faculty psychology is long past, it is still remarkably difficult to avoid talking about reason, emotion, or imagination and the distinctive role each has to play.[1] It is not desirable (perhaps not possible) to separate these various functions too sharply, but within such a wholistic anthropology it is instructive to single out the emotion of love particularly in its passionate expression and to examine its essential characteristics and functions as they relate to religious experience.

Questions about the meaning of love have been a preoccupation of philosophers, musicians, poets, theologians and ordinary reflective people since the dawn of civilization.[2] In our own time, however, exploration of the theoretical aspects of love has been singularly neglected by psychoanalysts, the biological and social sciences, historians, humanists and even theologians. No doubt Freud's negative evaluation of love has contributed to this neglect, but it remains surprising in view of its obvious importance in human experience. Poets and novelists have had to be the champions and standard bearers.[3]

The literature thins even more markedly when one turns to that expression of love known as passion. "Passion" is absent from subject catalogues in libraries, from titles of books and articles, and from indices where one would expect to find it. The Columbia Psychoanalytic Center in New York had no trouble funding symposia on individualism, narcissism and the limits of truth, but ran into difficulty when the topic was romantic love.[4] The researcher is forced to comb texts from a variety of disciplines in the hope of finding a chapter or paragraph dealing with passion.[5] Most often, the topic of passion comes up in discussions on affectivity, sexuality, romantic love, and sin or crime.

One obvious reason for the hesitancy to treat passion is the radically subjective nature of the experience. It is not easy to quantify or describe it in a neat or exhaustive way. But one must also point to a certain discomfort with the topic that makes scholars wary of undertaking any serious analysis of passion. The cultural and religious factors contributing to this state of discomfort are complex and their analysis beyond the scope of this essay. But one can surely identify in one's own experience some of the sources for fear and discomfort with regard to sexuality, that aspect of experience with which passion is most often connected.

For the moment, let us describe passion as any kind of feeling by which one is powerfully affected or moved, and turn to an examination of the roots of our understanding of passion in the west. A more comprehensive description of passion will follow.

SPIRITUAL PASSION: A HISTORY

Greek Roots

The meaning of passion has been massively influenced by Greek thought, especially that of Plato and his later interpreters. In what we might call the spirituality of ancient Greece, no aspect of life was *a priori* excluded. The sense of divine presence was universal. There were sacred places set aside as distinctively holy and used as sites for various cults, but in general the locus of the divine was the entire cosmos. No aspect of experience was excluded from the divine realm. This attitude perdured for centuries. We find the second century Neoplatonist, Plotinus, saying, "All the place is holy, and there is nothing which is without a share of soul."[6] E.H. Armstrong comments on this phenomenon, "When the perceived environment of worship was the whole town or the whole countryside, it was hardly possible for the worshippers to feel that they were a special flock, a people set apart, separate from the whole world of nature and the common society of humanity."[7]

In the Greek pantheon, passionate, sexual love was associated with Aphrodite, the goddess of love, and her son, Eros. In ancient religious thought, the world was born, not made, and reality sprang from the coupling of divine powers and sexual generation, giving these realities a distinctive importance.[8] Aphrodite and Eros are the embodiment of sexual charm, and of the excitement, sometimes leading to madness, that it produces. Their power is universal and includes the wilder and more disorderly passions as well as traditional mating and married love.[9] In ancient Mediterranean spirituality, "the wild as well as the tame, that which breaks all bounds and destroys all order as well as that which maintains order, had its place in the divine nature of things."[10] This full expression of love-madness was not a daily occurrence, but Aphrodite and Eros were felt to be present in the more ordinary and various expressions of sexual love as well.

Later philosophical forms of Greek piety took on a more austerely ethical nature that limited the unbridled expression of Eros. Yet Plato and his successors gave Aphrodite and especially Eros a very important place in their systems. "They saw that the passionate power of sexual love was essentially the same passionate power that drove the philosopher on in spiritual ascent to the Absolute Beauty and to God. But it was only at this highest level that it could be admitted."[11]

In the final scenes of the *Symposium*, Plato expresses most clearly his primarily negative assessment of passion. He banishes it from the human canvas since it brings in its wake nothing but untruth, pain, and destruction. The drunken, erratic passion of

Alcibiades is contrasted with the steady revealing power of Socrates' reason. There is no contest. Passion, like the artists who inspire it, must be forever banished if human happiness is to be achieved. While Plato does allow for what he calls "divine madness"— that turbulent side of love by which one is freed from the yoke of convention and freed for reunion with the One[12]—reason, not feeling, is the centerpiece of his thought.[13]

Aristotle takes Plato's emphasis on reason a step further. Aristotle distinguishes three types of love. The first is the love of utility in which one person loves another for her own personal benefit. The second is the love of pleasure in which persons love each other because it is pleasureable. In the third type of love, the only true friendship, one loves another because of who she is in herself. A true friend is one who cares about the welfare of the other person and wishes her well. Reason, not feeling, holds sway in this highest form of love.

Whereas Plato maintained the desiring love of *eros* at the heart of all love, Aristotle uses the term *philia* to describe genuine friendship and relegates *eros* to sexual love, placing the latter in a position inferior to the love of friendship. For Aristotle as well as for Plato, true love is governed by reasoned choice, not by feeling or passion. The Greek philosophical outlook regarded passion as a dangerous, less-than-human force that was to be controlled, circumscribed, and subordinated to reason in every possible way. The god-like quality of reason was the supreme value, and all of life was to be brought under its sway.

Christian writers took this Greek tradition, transforming it on some levels but on others embracing and enhancing the devaluation of human passion. Mysticism, the most intense expression of religious experience, was one of the few legitimate arenas in which Christians could experience passion. Physical, sexual passion was rejected. All forms of passion were spiritualized and attached primarily to persons' relationships with God. Contrary to the Greeks, Christians rarely valued passionate love among humans as a good in itself.[14] Since passion is a staple of the human condition, such a negative attitude inevitably produces a tension between this well-known experience and the demands of the Christian life as they have been laid down in the tradition. Few attempts to ameliorate this tension, i.e., to render it creative rather than destructive, have been successful.

Over the centuries, fear and mistrust of the passions grew to an extent that in retrospect many view as paranoic. While it is difficult to distinguish the various reasons for past cautious attitudes toward the power of the passions, it is imperative that we weigh critically the values of the past in the interest of the fullness of life in the present. Today, two millennia after Plato, we remain bound and conflicted by these tensions. But the task of growing in our understanding of passion and the invitation to return it to its rightful place in our lives remain. In this essay, we focus on the role of passion in that particular human experience we call "religious."

It is helpful at this point to clarify the meaning of the term passion. This is all the more important since the experience of passion is very personal, often elusive, and resists tight categorization. But it is possible to lay out the substance and basic parameters of the term. "Passion" encompasses a wide variety of meanings.[15] It refers to the suffering of pain, as in the passion of Jesus or the suffering of the martyrs. It names any painful disorder of the body such as illness. Second, "passion," as the word itself suggests, implies passivity, i.e., being acted upon by some external agency. The derivative, "compassion," implies the ability to suffer with another, to sympathize with another's distress and to desire its alleviation. Third, "passion" is most often connected with sexual desires and impulses or, less commonly, with a proneness toward hot-tempered irascibility. It can also be used more broadly to speak of an eager outreaching of the mind toward something, an overmastering zeal or enthusiasm for a particular object. Finally, the word "passion" is connected with love and romance, with strong amorous feelings or desires.

In the context of our topic, I define "passion" as an intense form of affectivity, especially of love and desire between God and the human person. In addition to the descriptor "intense," one thinks of "strong," "vehement," "enthusiastic," "ardent," "zealous." In other words, "passion" signifies an extreme form of affectivity. Further, I will posit that passion is a mysterious impulse toward human wholeness and freedom. The passionate experience has the potential to open up one's personality, to lead one toward fuller self-knowledge, and to contribute to the creation of a new self.[16] Passion functions to organize every aspect of an individual's life, allowing no compromise.[17] It creates a consuming longing in the lover that includes and extends beyond the beloved. While affect can be warm, passion is hot. It is often accompanied with sighs, tears, groanings. It almost always brings a pleasureable pain in its wake and often finds its apogee in ecstasy, i.e., being taken out of oneself and united with the beloved.[18]

Passion in Religious Experience

We have seen that for Plato the highest form of love is eminently rational, free from the disturbing influences of passion and sexuality. The object of this pure love is an impersonal ideal—Goodness itself. Love among humans has no place in this ethereal, idealized love. The primary difference in Christian love is that the object is no longer an impersonal ideal, but a personal God who is the fullness of love, in fact love itself.[19]

In Christianity, love of God is the primary love. Other persons and things are loved only as they reflect and lead to God. The experience of passion has been stripped of any bodily, material, human, sexual context, and becomes the center of a purely spiritualized, mystical love. As mysticism is an extreme and intense form of religious experience, so it became appropriate for Christians to connect with it that intense form of affectivity, namely passion.

Taken in itself, the connection established between mysticism and passion is a logical one. As we shall see, it set the scene for extraordinary religious experience and the literature describing it that is part of the glory of the western Christian tradition. What is problematic for us today is any accompanying exclusion or denigration of matter, of human love, and especially of the passion associated with sexuality. While "passion" is not a four-letter word, its reputation has been tragically sullied.

Rosemary Haughton is one of few theologians who has grappled with these issues. Her books *The Passionate God* and *On Trying To Be Human* are examples of her attempt to take passion seriously and to explore its connections with the gospel message.[20] In general, Haughton defines passion as the drive of powerful emotion toward the knowledge, and, in some sense, the possession of an object outside oneself.[21] The experience of passion can bring a sense of liberation from ordinary life, a profound increase in self-knowledge with its concomitant maturity, a renewed pattern of activity that perdures after the "feeling" of passion has passed, and a broadening of one's understanding of life beyond law and custom. All of this takes place in the context of relationship. The gospel calls us to be free to fall in love with other persons and she regards the sexual expression of passion as the "type" of all passion because it contains within itself, by nature, the conditions for its

9

own development toward wholeness, and needs no help from outside.[22]

In *The Passionate God,* Haughton sets out to discover the radical implications of the poetic and scandalous statement that God became, and remains, human.[23] Only a love of intense passion on God's part can account for this gift to the world. With the incarnation and resurrection of Jesus as fulcra, Haughton builds a theology with the help of the concepts and language of the romantic love tradition. Central to this tradition are the ideas of "breakthrough" and "exchange."

According to Haughton, the paradigm of "breakthrough" is the incarnation in which the divine breaks into the sphere of the human. This breakthrough has several consequences. One of the most important is that it makes nonsense of the division of reality into material and spiritual. Second, incarnation does not affect only human beings but "involves every level of reality from the most basic particles to the ultimate Being of God."[24] The incarnation makes holy all materiality and bodiliness.

Haughton further suggests that the medieval category of "being" rings in the modern ear as a static concept. It has what she calls a "stopped" quality. Therefore she prefers to talk about the totality of life in terms of "love" rather than in terms of "being," since love implies dynamic relationship. Love cannot be love unless it is given and received, i.e., "exchanged."[25] This exchange goes on everywhere, from the intimate recesses of the Trinity to the lowliest form of matter.

10

For Haughton, the language of romantic passion provides the kinds of "concepts, images and language tools which can enable us to articulate the theology of exchange."[26] The images of passion, she says, are images of love in action pointing to some kind of breakthrough to an encounter that is perceived as difficult.[27] It is not too difficult for us to imagine the person of Jesus, walking the earth in his gentle, determined, healing way. Nor is it difficult for most of us to imagine deity as infinitely loving creator of the universe. It may not even be hard for us to imagine the persons in the Trinity in some kind of close relationship. But a totally unimaginable oneness, a divine passion so intense that God *has* to be Jesus and a Jesus so passionate he *has* to be God— this is "so outrageous a demand on human intellect and human courage that there are only two possible responses: utter faith or utter rejection."[28]

Haughton writes about the passion God has for human persons. This divine love works for, in, through and between people, embracing the "entire, mysterious and infinitely complex system of inter-relationships which is creation."[29] In particular, she believes that we can gain some insight into the passion that drove God to become incarnate by looking carefully at the way people love people, especially as that love is passionate "because that kind of love tells us things about how love operates which we could not otherwise know."[30]

But in spite of this creative theological analysis of passion, questions about the role of passion perdure. Is it possible for us to benefit from learning about the passionate love of the mystics? Is it possible to rehabilitate sexual passion in a Christian context, to envision a harmony between intense sexual experience and the rest of one's life—including one's commitment to Christianity? Because passion is dangerous—and few would deny this—must it be banished from the realm?

Some persons react negatively to attempts to recover passion, fearing a loss of reason and an ensuing chaos. While it is a truism that one must be ever vigilant to protect reason, I think that in the west we have erred in the opposite direction. I search theological literature to find warnings about the sins of the intellect to match the seeming terror aroused by sins of feeling and passion! However, we do indeed need to guard against an understanding of affectivity that is narrowly sentimental, falsely grounded in an illusory dream world, maudlin or egotistically romantic.[31]

But is it possible to broaden the horizons of our understanding of passion? What are the ways in which the presence of passion can enhance one's existence? One takes it for granted that passion drives great warriors, poets, and lovers. Is passion the exclusive domain of such persons? Are such persons possessed of a certain personality structure that lends itself to living a life of intensity? Or can "passion" be understood on other levels so that ordinary people might expect and be open to the ways in which passion can be life-enhancing? For example, how might the presence of passion change our experience of marriage, learning, appreciation for nature, child-rearing, attitudes toward injustice? Might we ever arrive at the point at which a life devoid of passion, like the unreflected life, is a life not worth living?

MEDIEVAL WOMEN MYSTICS: PROLEGOMENA

The Role of Tradition

In this essay, we examine the role of passion in the writings of two medieval women. We turn to the past, or tradition, not as something "out there" upon which to gaze and about which to make judgments. What happened *then* is part of a process that ends up with us *now*. On the one hand, we mediate the tradition by making intelligent decisions about it, but, on the other hand, the tradition mediates us, i.e., our understanding of the tradition forms the basis of our own development. We are always in the stream of this process and development. At each stage in history, new information emerges. We need to be on the lookout for, and open to, this new data, and be willing to see how the tradition is changed by this new information or experience.

The presence of passion in descriptions of religious experience has been a constant throughout the Judeo-Christian tradition. The prophets express passion for justice (Is 56; Jer 21), the psalms overflow with passionate feeling, and Paul's letters reveal the intensity with which he preached the good news (1 Cor 15). From Psalm 63:

O God, you are my God, I seek you early
   with a heart that thirsts for you
   and a body wasted with longing for you,
   like a dry and thirsty land that has no water.
So longing, I come before you in the sanctuary
   to look upon your power and glory.
Your true love is better than life;
   therefore I will sing your praises.

But the Song of Songs is the paradigmatic biblical expression of passionate love between woman and man. We will examine several of its central images and themes.

The Song of Songs

Although we hold a broader understanding of passion than that reflected exclusively in sexuality, the bridal imagery of the Song is without a doubt the primary analogue for the experience of passionate love in the mystical tradition.

Over two thousand years ago a person from the Jewish community recorded some passionate sentiments about a couple in love. The Song of Songs is a poem made up of songs about intimate love. The editor probably contributed little to either the content or the organization of the poem. "Like stringing a necklace, he loosely put together folk lyrics of varying lengths which added different facets of beauty to the unifying theme."[32] Male and female voices alternate, but there is little concern for the sequence of ideas in arranging the stanzas.

14

Scholars argue about the reasons behind its inclusion in the canon, about whether its provenance is Egypt or Mesopotamia,[33] and about how we are to interpret it.[34] Ancient Judaism looked kindly on sexual passion in marriage, viewing it as one of God's many gifts of creation. Early Christianity, influenced by the dualism of Greek philosophy and Stoic disdain for passion, used allegory to eschew the physical dimension of passionate love in favor of a spiritual interpretation. Origen, the brilliant second century Christian writer, begins his commentary on the Song by insisting on the mature, *spiritual* nature of the passionate mystical experience. He counsels that readers should be beyond the stage at which they feel the passion of their bodily nature. Readers "must not take anything of what has been said with reference to bodily functions but rather employ them for grasping those divine senses of the inner man."[35] Bernard of Clairvaux offers a similar caution in his sermons on the Song: "Take heed that you bring chaste ears to this discourse of love; and when you think of these two lovers, remember always that not a man and a woman are to be thought of, but the Word of God and a Soul."[36] Bernard is also concerned to emphasize tender rather than passionate love:

> Christian, learn from Christ how you ought to love Christ. Learn a love that is tender, wise, strong; love with tenderness, not passion, wisdom, not foolishness, and strength, lest you become weary and turn away from the love of the Lord.[37]

15

Bernard was so interested in guarding against what he considered dangerous or sexual passion that he is not able to advert to the passionate dimension of his experience nor the passion implied in the erotic language he used to describe it.

The Greek and Latin fathers usually interpreted the bride in the Song as a communal entity, i.e., the church.[38] Medieval historians note a change to the personal dimension of the bride in terms of the individual monk or nun. Today there is general agreement that the original setting of the Song was one of celebration and no one gainsays the erotic character of the poem. Whether that eroticism belongs to the realm of the physical and sexual or to that of the spiritual and mystical—or to both—remains an open question. William Phipps comments, "It is one of the pranks of history that a poem so obviously about hungry passion has caused so much perplexity and has provoked such a plethora of bizarre interpretations."[39]

The text of the Song begins with the bride speaking:

I will sing the song of all songs to Solomon
     that he may smother me with kisses

Your love is more fragrant than wine,
     fragrant is the scent of your perfume,
and your name like perfume poured out;
     for this the maidens love you.
Take me with you, and we will run together;
     bring me into your chamber, O king.

The bridegroom responds:

> How beautiful you are, my dearest,
>> O how beautiful,
>> your eyes are like doves!
> How beautiful you are, O my love,
>> and how pleasant!

The senses of the bridegroom are filled with every detail of the beloved's beauty. He celebrates her beauty with impassioned praise:

> You have stolen my heart, my sister,
>> you have stolen it, my bride,
>> with one of your eyes, with one jewel of your
>>> necklace.
> How beautiful are your breasts, my sister, my
>> bride!
>> Your love is more fragrant than wine,
>> and your perfumes sweeter than any spices.
> Your lips drop sweetness like the honeycomb,
>> my bride,
>> syrup and milk are under your tongue,
>> and your dress has the scent of Lebanon.
> Your two cheeks are an orchard of
>> pomegranates,
>> an orchard full of rare fruits
> . . .
> My sister, my bride, is a garden close-locked,
>> a garden close-locked, a fountain sealed
>>> (Song 4:9–12).

In the Middle Ages, the Song of Songs was the most read and commented upon book in the Bible—by Jews and Christians alike.[40] Medieval monasticism had inherited from Origen (via Jerome) a threefold schema explaining and connecting three books from the wisdom literature—Proverbs, Ecclesiastes and the Song of Songs. These writings functioned to instruct persons in the three stages of the spiritual life. Proverbs, for beginners, taught one how to live virtuously. Ecclesiastes, for the more proficient, required that one despise the things of this world as vain and passing. The Song of Songs was for the advanced, instructing those far along on the mystical journey about the ways of love and union with God.[41] It was thought that great maturity was required for one to understand the Song correctly in its spiritual meaning.

Jean Leclercq explains the popularity of the Song as due to the prominence of an eschatological vision in the monastic community. The monks saw in the Song an expression of that intense desire for the fullness of beatitude awaited in eternity. "The Canticle is the poem of the pursuit which is the basis for the whole program of monastic life."[42]

It is clear that for the medieval mystics, the passion of the Song reflected only the pure, spiritual, and unsullied quest for God. They experienced the call of God as so intense, so burning that they became passionately caught up in receiving and responding to the touch of God. The language and images they used reflected passionate desire in the search for God.

As we will see below, some medieval women

mystics used the imagery of bride and bridegroom from the Song (along with other imagery) to express their passionate involvement with God. The relationship of spiritual passion to human passion was viewed on a hierarchical scale with sexual union at the bottom and spiritual union at the top. Today we aspire to a more inclusive hermeneutic that will account for the full range of experience in an integrative rather than in a hierarchical mode. William Phipps reminds us that the Song of Songs is the most sensuous book in the Bible and in all of antiquity. It speaks of the joy and constancy of genuine affection. It celebrates a bond that is sweeter than honey and stronger than a lion.[43] Roland Murphy speaks to the connections between human and divine love in the Song:

> The issue is not so much whether the Song deals with human love as opposed to divine love, as if these were two totally disparate things. It deals with love on various levels, and love belongs to both the human and the divine. If God is love, human sexual love must have some relationship to him; it reflects and participates in a divine reality. Both levels of love are to be retained in the perspective of the Song.[44]

With the imagery of the Song before us, we turn to the Middle Ages and the mystical accounts of Hildegard and Hadewijch.

We examine religious passion as it is expressed in the writings of two, still largely unknown, medieval women mystics, Hildegard of Bingen and Hadewijch of Antwerp.[45] If attention to the workings of passion among humans provides insight into the passion of God, so might attention to the religious experience of these women shed light on the potential of passionate experience in the many aspects of daily life. We focus on the meaning of religious passion as it is expressed in their theology, in their use of erotic language and imagery, and in manifestations of intense commitment or singleness of purpose.

We begin by asking about the reasons for the legitimacy of choosing women mystics as a resource in the search for the meaning of passion in religious experience. First, if mysticism is an intense form of religious experience, including the affective, it is likely to reveal in clearly delineated strokes the characteristics of passion.[46] At the same time, one must not allow the focus on mysticism to obscure the broader texture of one's entire experience as a disclosure of God's free generosity and our response to it.[47] It would be similarly inappropriate to regard passion as divorced from the milder, more routine experiences of affectivity in one's daily life.

Second, it is a commonplace that western culture recognizes a distinctive connection between affectivity and women. Women are seen to be familiar and at home with the ways of the heart. This has had both positive and negative ramifications. On the positive side, women's love is seen as superior, as godlike in its unconditioned character. Unfortunately, this kind of unconditional love is viewed almost exclusively in terms of motherhood, resulting in a disservice both to the values of motherhood and to those of romantic, erotic love. On the negative side, the identification of women with affectivity and erotic passion has caused women to be viewed as unreliable, fickle, and incapable of acting judiciously in a crisis or in serious human affairs. In the garden of Eden, Eve's intense desire for knowledge caused her to assent to the serpent's provocative invitation to partake of the fruit of the tree of good and evil—bringing catastrophe to the entire human race. In addition, portraits of the connection between women and affectivity too often deteriorate into exaggerated stereotypes. This is nowhere more evident than in some male historians' descriptions of women mystics whose prominence in the Middle Ages as visionaries is often attributed to "some kind of inherent female 'emotionalism.' "[48]

Third, the study of passion in women mystics is part of a larger feminist agenda that seeks to recover women's history and to bring to light women who can serve as models and heroines to enhance the lives of women and men today.

I concentrate on women mystics from the medieval period,[49] a period historians have characterized as an era that reflects strong emotion—a time of intense longing, fierce passion and ardent desire.[50] The medieval period may also be described as the golden age of women mystics.[51] The women who had access to education as well as to the means of recording their experiences—in many cases, a male amanuensis—were primarily anchoresses or members of monastic communities.[52] Therefore, it is to representatives of this group that we turn to discover the presence and role of passion revealed in the accounts of their religious experience.[53] We examine Hildegard of Bingen (twelfth century) and Hadewijch of Antwerp (thirteenth century).

HILDEGARD OF BINGEN

Life

Hildegard of Bingen—prophet, scientist, mystic, author, visionary, poet, dramatist and musician[54]—was the quintessential renaissance woman of the twelfth century and the first German mystic. Born the youngest of ten children in 1098 to Mechtild and the knight Hildebert von Bermersheim, Hildegard spent most of her life in the lovely Rhineland area of Germany. A precocious child, Hildegard began to see visions at a very young age. When she was eight she was sent to be tutored by Jutta von Spanheim who lived in a small cloister nearby. As a teenager, Hildegard chose to live under vows according to the Benedictine rule. In 1136 Jutta died, and at thirty-eight Hildegard was elected abbess of the growing group of women religious.

Hildegard was a contemporary and correspondent of Bernard of Clairvaux, Thomas Becket, a younger mystic, Elisabeth of Schönau, four popes (Eugene III, Anastasius IV, Adrian IV and Alexander III), and several royal families (Henry VI of Germany, Henry II and Queen Eleanor of England, the Emperors Conrad III and Frederick Barbarossa, and the

Empress Berta of Greece). She was involved in the major political and religious issues of her day—the crusades, the struggle between the empire and the papacy, and the Cathar heresy.

Hildegard's literary output is both prolific and diverse. Her first book, *Scivias,* a doctrinal work completed in 1151, takes its title from the exhortation, "Know the Ways of the Lord." This book was followed by a scientific and medical encyclopedia, *Nine Books on the Subtleties of Different Kinds of Creatures.* To this text was added a handbook of diseases and their remedies entitled the *Book of Compound Medicine.* She composed liturgical poetry and music, her songs being later compiled under the title *Symphony of the Harmony of Celestial Revelations.* In 1158 she began volume two of her visionary trilogy, the *Book of Life's Merits* on ethics, completed in 1163. Volume three, a scientific treatise written between 1163 and 1173, was titled *On the Activity of God.* Her corpus also includes many shorter occasional works, among them the lives of her patron saints, Rupert and Disibod.[55]

Hildegard's correspondence is impressive, spanning the last three decades of her life. She wrote to popes, emperors, prelates, abbots and abbesses, priests, monks and lay persons. She was acknowledged and revered in her own lifetime, receiving commendation from Pope Eugene III, Bernard of Clairvaux and many groups within the church. In spite of several severe illnesses, Hildegard managed to found two monasteries and completed four arduous preaching journeys.

The hints of passion in Hildegard's writings are

distinctive and instructive inasmuch as her style impresses the reader as eminently rational, subdued and orderly. In some ways she is the antithesis of her colleague, Bernard, whose mystical accounts overflow with intense erotic language and imagery. Hildegard describes her visions primarily in terms of light imagery, does not allude to ecstatic interludes, rarely addresses God in the second person, and overall pays little attention to the Song of Songs.[56] Her work is not marked by scholastic distinctions, apophatic negations, or descriptions of nuptial rapture. Yet she clearly communicates a sense of mystery and intense love.[57] We focus our attention primarily on her doctrinal work, *Scivias,* with occasional reference to other writings.

The *Scivias,* containing a Foreward and three parts, follows a trinitarian pattern. Part I reflects the work of God and the ways in which God relates to humanity and the world. Part II focuses on the Savior and relates the process of redemption. Part III takes as its theme the Holy Spirit, describing especially the role of the virtues in the journey of salvation. The text ends with an apocalyptic vision of the final judgment. Scholars contrast the tone of the *Scivias* in which Hildegard paints the image of a tumultuous world in flux with that of *On the Activity of God,* a structured, ordered account of the relations in the universe—a more delineated, detailed, and static image of the world verging on the mathematical.[58] For this reason, the *Scivias* appears as the most apt choice for our inquiry. My comments are organized under three general headings: the language, imagery and symbol of passion; incarnation; intensity of passion reflected in experience, commitment, or action.

LANGUAGE, SYMBOL AND IMAGE

Color and Light

In a first exposure to the *Scivias,* the reader is startled by the detailed imagery with which each vision begins. Brilliant colors abound—red, purple, green, as well as black and white.[59] The color green runs as a leitmotif throughout the text and symbolizes many things: the new growth and flowering in the spiritual life of those who follow the Word (II.6.26; III.10.4,7); the freshness of redemption (III.10.13); integrity of life (II.6.26); or even the deceits of the devil (III.11.27). The sensuousness of color is juxtaposed with frequent descriptions of light—Hildegard's favorite image. Light is described in varying degrees of shape and intensity and has as many meanings. She begins Part II of the *Scivias* with the following:

> I saw a very bright fire which was incomprehensible, inextinguishable, wholly living, and appearing as if it were totally alive. The flame of the fire was an airy color, and it was blazing violently in a gentle wind. . . . And I saw this flame lighten in color and give forth a bolt of lightning . . . the bright fire—blazing violently in a gentle wind . . . (II.1).[60]

The images of fire and light most often refer to the deity which Hildegard consistently discusses in trinitarian terms. She follows the tradition of associating fire with the Holy Spirit and light with the Word. Fire also represents the perfection of those who imitate the Word in their burning love (II.5.13).

Her account of the visions challenges readers to become involved with all their senses. Hildegard's descriptions are vivid, sensuous and intense, beckoning the reader to become involved similarly in an all-consuming and intense relationship with God.

Nature

In addition to the sensuous effect of the use of intense color, Hildegard employs a romantic view of nature to articulate her experience. One example of nature imagery appears in a letter Hildegard writes to Bertha, queen of Greece, who has written to Hildegard for counsel concerning her inability to conceive a child. Hildegard speaks to the queen about God's workings in terms of the cycle of nature.

> God's Spirit breathes and speaks: in wintertime, God takes care of the branch that is love. In summer, God causes that same branch to be green and to sprout with blossoms. . . .
> It is through the little brook springing from stones in the east that other bubbling waters are washed clean, for it flows more swiftly. . . . These lessons also apply to every

human being to whom God grants one day of the happiness and the glowing sunrise of glory. Such a person will not be oppressed by the strong north wind with its hateful foes of discord.

Hildegard then uses the imagery of romantic love, counseling the queen to look to the One who moves her, to sigh for the Divine. Hildegard closes with a prayer in which she describes God as a lover, intensely desiring to possess the queen as God's loved one: "May God grant you what you desire and what you pray for in your need, the joy of a son. The living eye of God looks on you: it wants to have you and you will live for eternity."[61] Hildegard's description of the idyllic natural setting sets the stage for the more personal love talk that follows.

Romantic Love

We have mentioned that Hildegard's works cannot be characterized in a primary way by the use of erotic imagery. Yet she uses such imagery at significant points throughout the text of *Scivias*. In each of the three parts, Hildegard ends the discourse on each vision with a refrain. In Part II God repeats the following:

Whereupon whoever sees with watchful eyes and bears with listening ears, this one may offer a kiss of love to my secret words, which flow from me, the living one.

In Part III, Hildegard has God repeat:

> Whoever has keen ears for understanding
> clearly, let this person pant for my words
> with a burning love of my image, and let this
> person write these words down in the con-
> sciousness of his or her soul.

It is as though she wants continually to call her readers back to the purpose of the spiritual life which is
affective, intense, and passionate. One is not permit-
ted to get lost for long in the complex intellectual
machinations of Hildegard's mind, for after each vision these refrains gently call the reader back to that
aspect of the divine that is erotic—a world of kissing
and panting for the Word of God.

In addition to the use of spousal imagery[62] in her
understanding of incarnation which will be treated
below, Hildegard also turns to courtly imagery in her
treatment of a theme that runs throughout her corpus—the intense struggle between good and evil.[63]
The Beloved is a counter force to evil. "I hurl Satan
down and hold the devil as irksome to myself, because
I desire the lover whom I embrace continuously and
whom I hold with joy in all things and above all
things" (III.6.6).

Spouses and Virgins

Most often, Hildegard echoes the patristic tradition that interprets the bride as symbol of the church.
But in other visions, the bride may represent the

Word, the individual soul, virgins, Mary or personified Wisdom.

The church is like an uncorrupted bride, betrothed to the most powerful king (II.5.1). In line with the common understanding of marriage in her day, Hildegard envisions the church as submissive and obedient to the bridegroom, receiving "his fertile donation of love for the procreation of children whom she leads to their rightful inheritance" (II.6.1). In Hildegard's eyes, the church was failing to carry out this duty of mediating salvation to the people. The divine voice she hears exhorts the church to be faithful to this responsibility:

> Let my Word be a bride to you for the restoration of my people. You may be their mother regenerating their souls through the salvation of the spirit and water (II.6).

Important to ecclesial purity is the presence of members dedicated to virginity. In this regard, Hildegard reflects the commonplace ambiguity of the Christian tradition about sexuality. She "oscillated between a joyful affirmation of the world and the body and a melancholy horror of the flesh—and its master, the devil" (III.4.17, 20). One is jarred by her "bold, affirmative view of sexual symbolism and a largely negative view of sexual practice."[64] The virgin is to be praised because she seeks the Word rather than an earthly husband. It is sinful for her to love anyone else more than the one to whom she is betrothed

(II.5.10f). The virgin is red as the dawn and burns as the flame of the sun (III.13.7).

Often in her writings, Hildegard juxtaposes earthly and heavenly love. Talk about passionate love for God is almost always predicated on one's success in despising the world and the desires of the flesh. The struggle to overcome the latter is pressing and difficult in Hildegard's eyes.

This earthly/heavenly dualism is also applied by Hildegard to lay and religious life. In a comparison of the two, Hildegard uses erotic imagery for the latter—one chooses religious over lay life because of the burning desire of one's will and the longing of one's soul (II.5.39). In a general letter directed to the laity, Hildegard has God speak words of chastisement and exhortation, words antithetical in tone to the lyrical strains of erotic love used to describe religious life. The distinctive role of the lay person is to be a servant of the law. In contrast, God says that religious "embrace Me with the kiss of love when for My sake they leave the world and by climbing the mountain of holiness become My beloved children."[65] In a later vision, Hildegard describes the virtue of chastity, taken by religious, in terms of the denial of human love.

> Chastity knows the self-denial of the flower of the flesh most keenly, just as a young maiden knows the burning of concupiscence but does not, nevertheless, look back at a man. She [chastity] has only the finest of desires and pants for her own sweet lover. Her love is the sweetest and most loving aroma of

31

all good things. Her lover delights in all of
the strength of steadfast virtue. Her lover
looks away from his own lovers to the inner
beauty of the soul (III.8.24).

For Hildegard, passions turned toward God be-
speak the height of religious intimacy. Passions turned
toward material reality are one of the major obstacles
to the spiritual life. Thus, Hildegard uses the same
erotic imagery to speak of the illicit lure of, and sinful
desire for, pleasure (that must be abandoned) as she
does to describe the glories of mystical experience in
which the lover finds it sweeter to pant for God, the
creator of all things (II.5.40). Passionate desire for
God is a crucial element of the spiritual life. The erotic,
sexual experience of panting for the beloved is not to
be repressed but directed toward God.

INCARNATION

The incarnation of the Word is a centerpiece in
Hildegard's theology. In one vision, God says,

People must never forget to call upon myself
alone, God, in these three persons. I showed
these three persons to people so that they
would burn most vividly in my love when I
sent the Word into the world because of my
love (II.2.3).

32

For Hildegard, faith appeared palely in the holy ancients under the old law, but then it appeared "burningly into the light with burning works when the Word of God was made flesh in an open manifestation" (III.2.1).

While light points to God, and fire and fervor to the Holy Spirit (III.4.12, 14), Hildegard reserves the most erotic imagery for the sending of the incarnate Word. In her description, "sweetness" takes on sensuous overtones: " . . . the incarnation of the Word dripped down the sweetest of tastes when the heavenly virtues built many buildings for the Word" (II.6.3.); and "then the entire earth was dripping with heavenly sweetness, and the bread of heaven remained in the world" (III.7.7). This sweetness makes it possible for creatures to return to the heavenly kingdom.

Hildegard also turns to the Song of Songs (2.4-5) to help her describe the incarnation: "The king led me into his wine cellar and put in order all the love that was in me. He revived me with flowers and refreshed me with fruit, for I was sick with love." The Son of God is the true vine that provides us with the best wine and orders our love. Love, she says, is like an unquenchable fire. It is from love for God that the sparks of true faith that burn in faithful hearts have their fire.[66]

Eucharist

At the eucharistic celebration, the offering of Christ's body and blood is drawn invisibly upward and God warms the offering with God's own warmth.[67]

This [offering] is the same as if some precious ointment were rolled into some bread and a sapphire were placed in some wine. I might whirl that around into such a sweet taste so that your mouth would not be able to distinguish that bread with the ointment nor that wine with the sapphire. But you would taste the sweet taste. My Only-Begotten is sweet and soft. What does this mean? My Only Begotten is symbolized in the ointment. . . . As a result, my Only-Begotten filled the wounds of people with sweetness so that they would not further decay . . . (II.6.13).

The body and blood of Christ are a source of forgiveness and of intoxication with charity for those who are dearest to God. The eucharist reminds Hildegard of this line from the Song of Songs (5:1): "Eat, my friends; drink and be intoxicated, my dearest ones" (II.6.21). The function of passion in these "dearest ones" is zealously to refrain from fleshly desires. In turn, God kindles in these souls the strongest virtues.

INTENSITY OF EXPERIENCE AND COMMITMENT[68]

Bodily Effects

Like most mystics, Hildegard experienced bodily effects from the intensity of her life with God. She was often ill, suffering at least three periods of extended and severe disability. In Hildegard's case, illness often appeared when she was prevented from executing what she believed was God's mandate for her. She was told to record her visions in writing, and until she finally undertook this task, she experienced violent illness. In the Introduction to the *Scivias,* Hildegard writes: "Eventually I started to write what I had searched out and come upon secretly. As soon as I did that, I became healthy with a received strength . . . and was able to bring my work to completion with difficulty, taking ten years."

A second example of the bodily effects of her relationship with God involves Hildegard's desire to move her convent from St. Disibod to Rupertsberg. The monks at Disibod tried to prevent it, fearing the loss of the fame and fortune that Hildegard brought to the monastery.[69] Hildegard made use of her family connections to secure the support of powerful and monied advocates, at the same time taking to bed with a paralyzing sickness that she ascribed to the delay in fulfilling God's will.[70] Hildegard's incredible will to carry out what she believed to be God's will brooked no obstacles.

Inner Effects

Finally, Hildegard's visions produced a profound inner effect as well. At the age of seventy-seven, Hildegard writes to Guibert of Gembloux, a Belgian monk, describing the spiritual awareness she had experienced since childhood. She calls it her *umbra viventis lucis,* the reflection of the living Light. In this vision that she saw day and night, her soul rose up

35

into heaven and spread itself out among different peoples who were far away from her in distant lands. She describes the inner effects of her vision of light.[71]

> Moreover, I can no more recognize the form of this light than I can gaze directly on the sphere of the sun. Sometimes—but not often—I see within this light another light, which I call "the living Light." And I cannot describe when and how I see it, but while I see it all sorrow and anguish leave me, so that then I feel like a simple girl instead of an old woman.[72]

Hildegard's visions result in a transformation of self. God's work in her makes of her a new creation.

Compassion for the Poor

For Hildegard, the ultimate act of illumination is compassion. The compassion of God is to be reflected in the compassion of the human community for the poor (III.10.26). Toward the conclusion of Part II of the *Scivias*, Hildegard turns to these themes. She counsels her readers to have compassion on those who possess nothing and warns them not to take pride in such activity.[73]

For all the mystics, the passion of their love affair with God is extended to others. When passion has had its rightful place in human life, one is better able to serve others with compassion, authenticity and spontaneity. The wholeness and truth of God can only be achieved in a shared life, so that the community of love which passion establishes between two must be realized in the wider community.[74] For Hildegard, one source and symbol of this compassion is the eucharist, a treasure held in one's bosom and heart that is to be distributed freely. She says, "You ought to overflow with generosity in your breast. . . . Yield yourself to God, and honor God with things 'from your substance' (Prov. 3:9)" (II.6.89).

Passion for Virtue

The larger context for this care for the poor is Hildegard's passionate concern with the virtues, especially for what she calls "justice." It is difficult to be precise about what Hildegard means by justice, since the term appears on almost every page of her corpus and she does not offer any systematic explanation of the term. But it seems safe to say that she is influenced by the biblical material on justice and the virtues as well as by the ways in which this material had been interpreted throughout the tradition.

At one point, she encourages a religious superior to allow God to kindle in her/him a thirst for the works of justice. She says, "And may the living Source intoxicate you out of the stream of divine delights with good and holy convictions."[75] In other circumstances, her concern for justice is extended to many different kinds of people. Toward the end of her life, the prelates of Mainz placed her community under interdict because she had given permission for a young excommunicated nobleman to be buried in the

37

church cemetery. The prelates wanted the body removed from the sacred ground. Hildegard refused, maintaining that the man had been privately reconciled before he died. She refused to back down in this struggle with the powers in the church, and the interdict—which denied her community its life blood, i.e., eucharist, communion, and the chanting of the divine office—was lifted only shortly before her death at eighty-one.

A second cause of Hildegard's passion for justice is the situation in the church of her day. Hildegard is both scandalized and outraged by what she considers to be the failure of the church to serve its people, to stand up for its true convictions and to confront the powers in the larger society that Hildegard saw as evil and as destructive of God's plan (III.11). Hildegard the reformer takes on the prophetic task with passionate intensity. Colloquially, one might say that Hildegard was a "one-tracker," i.e., a woman of single vision who never allowed herself to shrink from the prophetic word, nor retreat from the virulent struggle for good against the powerful forces of evil. But in the midst of the battle, Hildegard expresses a radical trust that the church, the bride of the Word, although weary, cannot be destroyed. "She will go forth pleasantly and sweetly to the embrace of her chosen one" (III.11.1).

On the individual level, she exhorts persons to live lives of intense virtue. She often contrasts the ideal of commitment to virtuous action with the biblical image of being lukewarm. In a famous passage in the *Scivias,* Hildegard saw men and woman carrying

38

vessels of milk and making cheeses. The milk represents human seed and the cheese stands for the human beings made from it.

> Some of the milk was thick, from which
> strong cheese was being made. This means
> the seed which, assembled and tempered use-
> fully and well in its strength, brings forth
> strong people, endowed with a great radi-
> ance of spiritual as well as carnal gifts . . .
> (I.4.13).

Other, less fortunate people are made from thinner milk—"stupid, lukewarm, and useless to God and the world" because they do not vigorously seek God. A third group, made from bitter cheese and spoiled milk, are unable to raise their minds to heaven. Only with grace and arduous effort can they win the victory.[76] Finally, Hildegard speaks of those people who are holy in body but not in mind. "They are like a lukewarm wind. . . . They are neither hot nor cold, because they do not have the necessary heat in their soul so that they can persevere in the control of the virginity they have begun" (III.10.8).

Friendship

One cannot help but wonder about the quality of personal relationships of one who is so obviously driven by a passionate love of God. Hildegard's letters reveal some hints of the kinds of personal relationships she had, yet she tells us little of her own personal feelings toward others. An exception was her relationship with a sister who was her secretary, Richardis von Stade. In 1151, Richardis, encouraged by her mother, her brother who was the archbishop of Bremen, and other church dignitaries, accepted the position of abbess of a convent at Bassum. Hildegard violently opposed the move. One may conjecture that her motives involved a combination of deep affection for this woman and of disappointment at losing a trusted assistant during a very busy and tumultuous time in Hildegard's life. She wrote in protest both to the officials involved and to Richardis. In a letter to the latter she says,

> I loved the nobility of your ways, your wisdom and chastity, your soul and all your life, so that many said: "What are you doing?" Now may all lament with me, all who have woe like my woe, who in the love of God bore such love in their heart and their mind for a person, as I had for you—one snatched away from them in an instant, just as you were taken from me.[77]

Later, a penitent Richardis decided to return to Hildegard, but sudden death prevented her. Her brother, the archbishop, wrote to Hildegard to tell her of Richardis' death. Hildegard sends a reply to the archbishop lamenting that while the world loved Richardis' intelligence and beauty, God loved her even more: "Therefore he did not want to surrender his Beloved to that inimical lover, the world. . . . And I too dispel from my heart the pain you have prepared for me through this daughter of mine."[78]

CONCLUSION

As we might have expected from a holy woman of the twelfth century, Hildegard channels her passion into the spiritual realm. Denial and denigration of physical passion and exclusion of the laity from the heights of religious experience go hand in hand with the choice for God. But we need not let this dualism and elitism blind us to the compelling expression of passion visible in the accounts of her life experience.

Her passion is in large measure intellectual in nature and oriented toward just action. She points us toward a wholistic understanding of religious experience in which both head and heart partake in an intense orientation toward God. Hildegard also nudges us to renew our own singleness of purpose in the quest for a just world. She leaves no opening for a sentimental kind of love affair that is not borne out in action on behalf of the other. Yet she does rely on the erotic imagery of the Song of Songs at key points in her account and she does employ erotic symbolism to express various aspects of the spiritual life. Her words invite us to examine the flame of our own passionate love for God, others and the world.

Hildegard's passion is prophetic. She sees sin and evil in vivid ways and is enflamed to confront, to chastise, to encourage, to fight. Her passion is the familiar passion of the reformer. Second, her passion is moral.

The pervading insistence with which she treats the virtues provides abundant evidence. At times her single-minded enthusiasm causes her to sound harsh, but behind the clear call to virtue lies a loving God who expressed a passionate love beyond imagining in the incarnation and in the Holy Spirit. Third, her passion was relational. She saw herself as the bride of the Word, but she is more concerned with the welfare of the church to which she is committed. We saw evidence of her passionate concern for the prosperity of her monasteries and those within them, and in a special way for Richardis, her secretary. She spends herself writing letters and preaching in order to assist others in their journey to God. She dearly desires that all believers be filled with goodness and be motivated to act in a loving and just manner.

We end with the closing words of the *Scivias*, words overflowing with erotic and sensuous imagery, words that capture the glory of the spiritual life as Hildegard experienced and understood it.

And whoever has tasted the mystical words of this book and placed them in her memory, let her be like a mountain of myrrh and frankincense, and all the other aromas. Let her ascend by means of many blessings from blessing to blessing, just as Abraham did. Let the new wedded bride of the lamb join that column to herself in the sight of God. And let the shadow of the hand of the Word protect her (III.13.16).

HADEWIJCH OF ANTWERP[79]

Life

Little is known about Hadewijch. Unlike other medieval women mystics whose lives were recorded, we have no "Life" of Hadewijch, but her familiarity with chivalry and courtly love and her knowledge of scripture and the fathers of the church, as well as her obvious education in Latin, rhetoric, numerology, astronomy, music, verse and French, suggest that she was an educated member of the upper class. Her life and her writing (*Poems in Stanzas, Poems in Couplets, Visions* and *Letters,* written between 1220 and 1240) were known in the fourteenth century, but by the sixteenth century her work seems to have been forgotten. In 1838, her corpus was rediscovered by three Belgian scholars.[80] A foremost contemporary scholar of Hadewijch, Paul Mommaers, calls her "the most important exponent of love mysticism and one of the loftiest figures in the Western mystical tradition."[81]

Hadewijch was not a nun, but belonged to a popular and widespread movement begun in the late twelfth century whose members called themselves beguines.[82] Beguines were urban women from various social classes who lived a loosely structured religious life adapted to different social circumstances and locations. Geographically, they were centered in northern France, Flanders and southern Germany. These pious women lived in their own homes, usually grouped near to each other, agreed to a regimen of prayer, asceticism, almsgiving and service (usually teaching and nursing), and obeyed a woman chosen as leader from among them. They maintained property and were self-supporting, often as cloth makers. Beguines practiced chastity while members of the group, but did not take solemn vows and were free to leave and get married at any time.[83]

The gradual hardening of church structures in the twelfth and thirteenth centuries put the beguines in jeopardy since they had no formalized rules, nor were they subject to local ecclesiastical authority through organized structures. The growing hierarchical suspicion of the extreme poverty of the Franciscans, the desire to have rigorous control over all forms of lay piety—especially that of women—and the fear of heresy all worked against them. The beguines were not without powerful supporters, but often suffered from the church's fears. When heresy could not be proved against them, they were often accused of laziness or illicit begging.[84]

From clues in Hadewijch's writing, one can surmise that she had either founded or joined a small group of pious women and had become its mistress. She believed that the young women in her group were specially called to the mystical state, even though they often failed to live up to her expectations. A number of factors—her high standards, opposition from within and outside of the community, jealousy, and an accusation that she was teaching quietism—led to her being evicted from her community and exiled. It is suggested that when she became homeless she offered her services to a leprosarium or hospital for the poor, enabling her to have a place to sleep and access to the chapel that was always a part of such establishments in her time.[85]

Hadewijch's Love Mysticism

Hadewijch is one of the foremost representatives of *minnemystiek* (love mysticism) to which women made an impressive contribution in the thirteenth century. She is also significant for Dutch literature inasmuch as her *Poems in Stanzas* are among the very few extant Middle Dutch love songs in the troubadour tradition of courtly love, and her prose, along with that of the Cistercian mystic Beatrijs of Nazareth (c. 1200-1268), is the earliest extant prose in the vernacular.[86] Hadewijch does not treat love in a systematic fashion, but the word occurs on almost every page of her writing and is obviously the controlling concept in her spirituality.

There is some debate about what "love" (*minne*) means for Hadewijch. Since she infrequently refers to Christ or to bridal imagery, one concludes that Hadewijch understands "love" as experience rather than as a personification of God or Christ.[87] De Paepe, a Hadewijch scholar, distinguishes three basic moments in Hadewijch's experience of *minne:* the awareness of a distance between *minne* and herself, the complete surrender to *minne*, and restored balance.[88] We will be

45

able to test this hypothesis in our examination of the expressions of passion in Hadewijch's *Poems in Stanzas,* written for the beguines in Hadewijch's community, and in occasional references to other writings.

We choose *Poems in Stanzas* in order to focus this study, but more importantly because all forty-five poems are in the tradition of courtly love.[89] "The imagery of courtly love—the unattainable lover, the submissive service to love, the complaints, the hope and despair, the all-pervading power of love—provides the poems with a strong thematic link."[90] But, as we will discover, this literary imagery takes on a new and existential spiritual significance in Hadewijch. The "lady" in the courtly love tradition becomes God or Love to whom the soul offers the service of love. At times Hadewijch becomes the knight errant, courting dangers and adventures for Love's sake. Mommaers calls these poems "mystical love lyrics"—a new genre created by Hadewijch and characterized by lyrical genius.[91] In addition, the impact of romance on this type of poetry is well established, making it apt for our inquiry.[92]

We examine Hadewijch's love poetry under four headings: the relation of passion to reason; her emphasis on the humanity of Jesus; the pain involved in passionate love; the effects of passionate love—the transformed self.

The Role of Reason

Although one is almost overwhelmed by the intense, erotic tone of Hadewijch's writing (in stark contrast to Hildegard), she does not disdain reason. She describes reason as noble, as that part of a person that is renewed and enlightened as a result of the ecstatic, affective mystical experience.[93] Reason has the all-important function of keeping one's eyes on the truth. "Thunder is the fearful voice of threat . . . and it is enlightened reason which holds before us the truth, and our debt . . . and our smallness compared to Love's greatness" (Letter 30).

Hadewijch is not naive about the possible risk to Love that Reason can bring, but she knows that Love without Reason is incomplete (30.9).[94] Sensuous, hedonistic persons do not want to consult Reason, preferring to immerse themselves in pure pleasure. But pleasure is not the only aspect of Love. After promising marvelous things and bestowing initial joy, Love can run away and leave the lover abandoned. Further, Reason reminds Hadewijch that she is a human being and therefore not capable of experiencing the fullness of Love for which she hungers so intensely. At first she thinks Reason is just picking a feud with her, but then realizes that it was Reason who taught her to live the truth (30.11). Reason also has a key role in the process of discernment, so important to the spiritual life (Letter 24). Hadewijch places her experience of mystical love within the context of truth and of the totality of the human person. A love cordoned off from the other aspects of her existence cannot be authentic.

Above all for Hadewijch, Reason brings understanding to the experience of passion (9.9). Reason illuminates the entire abyss of Love and gives its approval and counsel to scrutinize, with Love, the whole garden of Love (19.5). Reason safeguards Hadewijch's love affair with God from being enclosed within itself. Reason leads her to see the point, the goal of Love. "For no one can become perfect in Love unless he is subject to his reason" (Letter 13). She knows that even though it has a separate function, passionate love is incomplete without Reason. Reason makes it possible to receive the completion or the fruition of Love, and also *to know* how this is in fact so (30.14). Hadewijch does not covet this discovery for herself. She knows that it is gift and prays that all those who love may win the favor of Reason. She says, "In winning the favor of Reason/Lies for us the whole perfection of Love" (30.15). The pearl of great price is Love, but Love without Reason is ripe for deception.

But reason is not infallible. It too is subject to error, and when it errs the results are far-reaching. The will becomes weak and lazy; the memory loses its deep notions, its joyous confidence and its zeal to do good. The noble soul becomes depressed, requiring it to obtain its consolation from bare hope (Letter 4). Nor does Hadewijch ignore the tension she feels between the two powers and their differing objectives. But rather than sacrifice one or the other for a false peace, she resigns herself to allowing both to have their say.

> The loving soul wants Love wholly, without
>   delay;
> It wishes at all hours to delight in sweetness,
>   In opulence according to its desire.

Reason commands it to wait until it is
    prepared;
But liberty wishes to lead it instantly
    Where it will become one with the Beloved.
    Storms of this kind
    Impart a calm resignation (15.5).

It is agony for the passionate soul to wait, and Hadewijch finds the counsel of Reason cruel and confusing
(16.3). She is relentlessly honest in describing the full
range and at times the conflicting aspects of her experience of Love.

Hadewijch offers a poetic summary of the way
she understands the relationship between love and
reason. Since she says it so well, I have chosen to cite a
lengthy section. Reason and love have distinctive functions, but charity is the unifier:

The power of sight that is created as natural
to the soul is charity. This power of sight has
two eyes, love and reason. Reason cannot see
God except in what he is not; love rests not
except in what he is. Reason has its secure
paths, by which it proceeds. Love experiences failure, but failure advances it more
than reason. Reason advances toward what
God is, by means of what God is not. Love
sets aside what God is not and rejoices that it
fails in what God is. Reason has more satisfac-
tion than love, but love has more sweetness
of bliss than reason. These two, however, are
of great mutual help one to the other; for

reason instructs love, and love enlightens reason. When reason abandons itself to love's wish, and love consents to be forced and held within the bounds of reason, they can accomplish a very great work. This no one can learn except by experience (Letter 18).

Finally, no matter how great her disappointment at Love and no matter how deeply Reason has wounded her, she does not abandon the path of passionate attachment to Love. The setbacks do not lead her to close herself off from the experience of passion, but in a way increase her resolve to continue on this path. She says:

> No matter how Love has disappointed me,
> I must yet follow her,
> For she has utterly engulfed
>   My soul, from the depths of my heart.
> I will follow her totally (30.13).

She has the courage in the midst of the difficulties of Love to persevere. She is willing to admit that Love enflames her whole being and calls her to be faithful.

Depending on one's historical perspective or particular personality structure, one may choose to emphasize reason or intense love. While there is no dearth of examples of passion run amok because divorced from reason, social and religious understanding has generally made passion suspect and given free reign to reason. But if one agrees that passionate love needs some belated but legitimate attention, one must also admit that nothing is gained by disparaging or ignoring the function of reason. For it is the whole person who lives and loves and thinks and makes decisions. Hadewijch was ahead of her time both in the freedom with which she embraced and talked about passionate love of God and for God, and in her understanding that passion need not be cooled or distorted by reason.

THE HUMANITY OF JESUS

Hadewijch's writing resounds with the conviction that mystical union with God is lived here on earth as a love relationship. Since she does not often speak of Christ in *Poems in Stanzas,* we need to turn to her *Letters* and *Visions* to discover the role of Christ in her mystical experience.

Throughout these writings, Hadewijch speaks consistently of God in trinitarian terms, but Christ is given a distinctive role. When Hadewijch speaks of union with God she almost always means the God-man.[95] Additionally, Hadewijch places in the foremost position the humanity of Christ. Without conformity to Christ's humanity, conformity to the divinity is not possible. As we will see below, she sees conformity to Christ's humanity as the motive force behind leading a virtuous life.[96] But she exhorts her readers "to live Christ" in the fullest sense, participating with the totality of one's being in the totality of Christ. Each mystery of Christ's life—annunciation, nativity, flight into Egypt, pain, poverty, ignominy, being forsaken yet remaining compassionate—is an invitation to imitate him, to enter into comparable experiences in our own lives.

Of all the mystics, Hadewijch conveys beyond any doubt that she experiences the human person Jesus as a man.[97] Further, her descriptions leave little doubt about the passionate nature of her love affair with the God-man. But she refuses to let go of either the divine or the human in God. The truth of both is found in one single fruition. This unity is evident in many of her descriptions. In Vision seven, she says:

> I desired to have full fruition of my Beloved, and to understand and taste him to the full. I desired that his Humanity should to the fullest extent be one in fruition with my humanity, and mine then should hold its stand and be strong enough to enter into perfection until I content him, who is perfection itself, by purity and unity, and in all things to content him fully in every virtue. To that end I wished he might content me interiorly with his Godhead in one spirit and that for me he should be all that he is, without withholding anything from me.[98]

The occasion for such intimate union with Christ for many medieval women mystics was the reception of communion during the eucharist. In the seventh vision, Hadewijch offers this powerful erotic description of her experience of union.

> After that he came himself to me, took me
> entirely in his arms, and pressed me to him;
> and all my members felt his in full felicity, in
> accordance with the desire of my heart and
> my humanity. So I was outwardly satisfied
> and fully transported.

After a short while, Hadewijch loses sight of the out-
ward manly beauty and begins to merge with her Beloved. "Then it was to me as if we were one without
difference."

At all stages of the love relationship, Hadewijch
speaks of the desire to "content" the Beloved.

> What I most desired,
> Since Love first touched my heart,
> Was to content her
> According to her wish (16.9).

Hadewijch's poetry conveys how her entire being
aches to please the beloved. Persons in love understand this desire clearly. In all forms of intense love,
the lover wants nothing more than to have the beloved enjoy whatever gives her/him happiness. In
turn, the lover experiences great joy when he is able
to content the loved one. And yet in Hadewijch's experience with God she understands clearly that "No living man under the sun/Can content Love" (20.1). But
this truth does not cool the flames of her love. She has
been captured by love and gives in willingly to its
demands and sufferings.

We close this discussion of Hadewijch's account

of her relationship with Jesus with several stanzas
from Poem 20 which describe the sublime nature of
love. These stanzas are representative of the intense
erotic nature of Hadewijch's description of her love
affair with God.

God, who created all things
And who, above all, is particularly Love,
I supplicate to consent,
    According to his pleasure,
That Love now draw the loving soul to herself
    In the closest union possible to Love.

The union possible to Love is very close,
But how close, I am the one who does not
    understand.
But he who is ardent for the sake of Love
    Shall yet understand
How Love is always possessed in violent
    longing:
    Here one cannot find repose.

. . .

All who love must be moved to pity
That Love lets me moan thus
And cry so often: "Woe is me!"
    In what season and when
Will Love reach out to me
    And say: "Let your grief cease"?
    "I will cherish you;
I am what I was in times past;

Now fall into my arms,
And taste my rich teaching!" (20.5, 6, 12).

The desire for Love is intense and persistent. Even in
the midst of pain and suffering and violent longing,
Hadewijch never gives up. In the midst of the tur-
moil, she hears the clear voice of Godly assurance—"I
will cherish you . . . fall into my arms." She portrays
the complex experience of passionate love accurately,
poetically, and with great feeling. She is obviously
deeply immersed in the experience of Love and yet is
able to find language that brings to life for others this
most intimate of human experiences.

THE WOUND OF LOVE

The pleasures and promises of Love are not en-
joyed without cost. Pain, wounding, imprisonment,
violence and despair dot the landscape of Hadewijch's
love affair.

He who serves Love has a hard adventure
Before he knows Love's mode of action,
    Before he is fully loved by her.
    He tastes her as bitter and sour;
    He cannot rest for an instant (2.4).

In these *Poems in Stanzas,* Love has a fickle side. At
times, Love gives consolation and health, at other
times she administers heavy blows and wounds (3.5).
Love's arrow strikes and "At all times when the arrow

strikes/It increases the wound and brings torment"
(14.3; 43.12). The theme of pain and joy intermin-
gled (3.6), so common in the literature of passionate
love, runs as a leitmotif through Hadewijch's poetry.
Truth is revealed in "sweet pain" (12.4); exile is sweet
(9.3); and she lives "with a sad heart, joyful" (13.1).
Being in love is also an imprisonment. However,
brave knights "ever serve in the chains of Love"
(10.3), and Love makes even imprisonment sweet.

> That is mighty Love's mode of action:
> If she wholly lures someone to her hand,
> Although she forces him with violence,
> She contents him and sweetens his chains
> (19.11).

Love initially sweeps Hadewijch off her feet and
then withdraws hiding herself. This feeling of aban-
donment by Love may be connected with Hadewijch's
being rejected by her community and left to wander
alone. One of her keenest sufferings is that of feeling
like an alien, an exile in her own land (4.9). In other
instances she speaks of her oppressors, perhaps her
once loving sisters, as aliens. She is puzzled and worn
down by all her grief. She says,

> So greatly has the pain of love worn me out
> That I am now unfit for anything (2.8).

Hadewijch is puzzled by what she perceives to be
the intense agony of her lot. She does not suffer the
ordinary round of upsets and discontents but experi-

ences extreme and intense forms of suffering. These experiences reflect a violence rarely spoken of so directly in the mystical literature. She says,

> O what did I do to good fortune
> That it was always so merciless to me?
> That to me it did such violence—
> More than to a thousand other souls (3.2)?

Using the imagery of the courtly love tradition, Hadewijch laments that her shield has warded off so many stabs that there is no room left on it for a new gash (3.3). Even her longing for love takes on violent dimensions.

> The union possible to Love is very close,
> But how close, I am the one who does not
>   understand.
> But he who is ardent for the sake of Love
>   Shall yet understand
> How Love is always possessed in violent
>   longing:
> Here one cannot find repose (20.6)

She wishes that she could understand her "losses, defamations and oppressions" as good but she does not have the wisdom (3.4).

At moments, Hadewijch seems near despair, but she perseveres. She addresses Love:

> Alas, Love! You have long driven me to
>   extremity;

But in this very extremity to which you have
    driven me,
I will keep vigil, Love, in service of your love
    (43.14).

But in the long run, Love is faithful to Hadewijch. She
suffers gladly knowing that Love has never revoked
her promises (2.8). Love honors her friends and can be
counted on even though she causes "smarting pain"
(2.10). Hadewijch will "endure Love's storms with confidence" (2.11).

    The deep suffering that Hadewijch describes is an
inescapable component of her passionate love affair
with Love. Although historical evidence is inconclu-
sive, one may surmise that her descriptions of spiritual
pain are intimately connected with the actual rejection
and suffering that she knew during her lifetime. She
was forced to wander as an alien with nowhere to lay
her head, and this situation may have even been
caused in part because of her unwillingness to compromise the intensity of her singleness of purpose.

    But at a more profound level, one can reflect on
the inevitable onslaught of suffering experienced
whenever one chooses to become vulnerable, to open
oneself to the gift of passionate love. In addition to the
joyful wounding of the love experience in itself, there
are other sources of pain. The "other" is given permission to enter deeply into the lover's psyche. This
requires revelations of self and adjustments to accom-
modate the other that are often painful. Second, in
passionate love, one allows oneself to become intensely
caught up in the beloved and her/his affairs. This cre-

ates another kind of vulnerability that opens one to being wounded. The stance of passion is never the cool, safe, detached position of the disinterested onlooker. Third, the lovers become one in a way that causes the pain and suffering of one to be deeply felt by the other. Often the most painful form of suffering occurs when one is unable to relieve the suffering of the beloved, resting content to stand by in silent support.

Hadewijch gives witness to a love that perseveres in the midst of intense suffering. She is not timid about her lamentations, but the flame of her desire is not made dim by hardship. The vision of her beloved Love and the promise of joyful fulfillment are always before her, leading her on and giving her strength in the midst of adversity.

THE TRANSFORMED SELF

We come now to the final and most important aspect of Hadewijch's passionate love affair with God, i.e., the transforming effects wrought in her. The proof of authenticity in the spiritual life is the quality of life that flows from it. As one becomes more deeply attuned to life "in Christ," the dispositions, choices and activities of life increasingly reflect the life of the Beloved. Such actions are grounded in the new identity that emerges from a passionate encounter with God. In a very real sense, one becomes and continues to become a new person, a new creation.

The call of passion occurs at different stages in one's life. Recent psychological analysis of the "stages of life" suggests that passion is more likely to knock on one's door at certain pressure points along life's continuum, e.g., adolescence or mid-life. But reflection on the utter complexity of life leads one to acknowledge that the call of passion can occur at any time and in any circumstance. Each person must identify the contours of her/his distinctive knock.

Too many of us are probably too busy and distracted even to recognize the knock when it occurs. Others suppress the call quickly for a variety of reasons—fear or inconvenience perhaps. Yet others will do battle with passion. The outcomes vary. One may succeed in overcoming the drive toward passion, or passion may be the victor in a harmful way leading toward misery and destruction. Haughton contends that it is not possible simply to reject the call and go on as before. The defenses one has built up must either be strengthened or abandoned. In the first instance, prejudices and habits of thought that were taken lightly must assume the force of fixed immovable truths in order to be strong enough to repel the invasion of passion. Hadewijch says of this option:

> All who shun this renewal
> And renew themselves with newness not that of
> Love
> Shall be distrusted by the new,
> And condemned by both the new and the
> newly reborn (7.7).

The second instance is the optimal course and involves opening oneself to the self-knowledge and integrating power that the experience of passion makes available.[99] The experience of passion can lead to becoming a new creation, a new person who is both more profoundly human and holy.

Hadewijch was not afraid to open the door to passion and to its renewing power. That this is so is evident in every line of her poetry. We give but one example.

> Oh, how sweet is proclaiming the renewal!
> Although it occasions new vicissitudes
> And many new sufferings,
> It is a new security;
> For love will truly repay us
> With great new honors;
> Love shall cause us to ascend
> To Love's highest mystery.
> Where that new totality shall be
> In glorious fruition,
> And we shall say, "New Love is wholly mine!"
> Alas, this newness happens too seldom! (7.7)

We discuss the textual evidence for Hadewijch's transformation under the following headings: her use of nature imagery; the experience of surrender; the virtuous life; her joy and optimism.

Nature Imagery

Faithful to the tradition of the troubadours, Hadewijch deftly weaves the symbols of nature and the seasons throughout her tale of love. Hadewijch's graphic

depiction of the renewal of nature points to the many
levels of renewal of her human and spiritual life. Even
though it may be winter for her as she writes, she keeps
her eye on the promise of spring. Days grow longer;
hazelnut trees blossom; sap flows upward from the
roots; meadow and plant don their foliage; birds grow
joyful and sing; roses appear between thorns; flowers
open wide and take on transforming color; storms give
way to fair weather.

Nature signs the newness of love. In Poem seven
she writes:

> Oh, Love is ever new,
> And she revives everyday!
> Those who renew themselves she causes to be
>   born again
> To continual new acts of goodness.
> How, alas, can anyone
> Remain old, fainthearted at Love's presence?
> Such a person lives truly old in sadness,
> Always with little profit;
> For he has lost sight of the new path,
> And he is denied the newness
> That lies in new service of Love,
> In the nature of the love of new lovers (7.3).

In the midst of her anguish, Hadewijch experiences
spring as promise and trusts that her own renewal
will emerge more tangibly as does the renewal of
nature each year. But on occasion, the reader also
glimpses hints of a renewal that is a present reality as
well. She says,

The new year already begins.
For anyone who has resolved
To spare neither much nor little
For Love, his pain becomes pure profit (33.2).

In another vein she prays that others may know renewal.

May new light give you new ardor;
New works, new delights to the full;
New assaults of Love, new hunger so vast
That new Love may devour new eternity!
     (33.14).

Hadewijch's lyrics bring nature to life as sign and symbol of the renewal that divine love promises. For her,
nature serves as a troth from the Lord. Her response
is to trust in God's fidelity.

Surrender

As we have seen, one is free to respond to the call
of passion or to reject it. The possibility of renewal
through passion is not automatic or magical, but de-
pends on the choice to abandon oneself to its power.
It is obvious that Hadewijch chooses to surrender herself to Love. The theme runs as a refrain throughout
the *Poems*.

A word of caution is in order here. Women writing today about their experience warn of the dangers
of choosing self-surrender precipitously. Culturally,
surrender has been associated with women in a par-

ticular way. The sexual act has been one-sidedly inter-preted, becoming the paradigm for male initiation and action and for female reception and surrender. But the problems inherent in any discussion under-taken by women about surrender must not blind us to its positive role in human and religious experience. The essence of the Christian myth involves laying down one's life in love and freedom for another. But it is critically important that women especially under-stand the complexity and nuances of this act, making sure that the prior work involved in having a life and being free is well on its way before one begins to talk about surrendering it.

Hadewijch is clear about her choice to surrender to Love's demands. She says, "Alas, I gave full trust to Love,/Since first I heard her named,/And I left myself to her free power" (1.4). In fact, in her mind, this choice is the very reason why everyone around her wishes to condemn her (1.4). Hadewijch defers to Love, makes herself continually available to Love (36.2), trusting that Love is wise and knows best—whether Love's decision is to scourge or pardon (1.6, 8). She prays that Love dispose of her freely accord-ing to her pleasure (2.9; 3.2).

> I do not complain of suffering for Love:
> It becomes me always to submit to her,
> Whether she commands in storm or in stillness
> (22.4).

Whether one agrees with her or not, one must admit that Hadewijch speaks with honesty and abandon of her experience of radical loss of self that accompanies her involvement with God. The sexual overtones are unmistakable even though she speaks of a spiritual experience:

> This is the best counsel
> > That can be given on the subject:
> > To one whom Love has thus captured
> > And bound with her chains,
> > That he surrender himself into her hands
> > And always be submissive
> To all the lordship that Love exercises;

> . . .

> > Love has subjugated me:
> > To me this is no surprise,
> > For she is strong and I am weak.
> > She makes me
> > Unfree of myself,
> > Continually against my will.
> She does with me what she wishes;
> Nothing of myself remains to me;
> > Formerly I was rich,
> Now I am poor: everything is lost in love (24.4,
> > 5).

Hadewijch places before the reader the terror of passionate love. The risk of loss of self is real, and one is foolhardy to ignore the seriousness of the stakes that are involved. And yet the loss of the old self is a *sine qua non* of the emergence of the new. Hadewijch is forced to leave her former life and friends behind because she wishes to live freely and receive great riches and knowledge from Love. She is very sure of herself here. She says, "He who disputes them with me has it on his conscience./ I cannot do without this gift,/I have nothing else: I must live on Love" (24.6).

But surrender has further dimensions to it. It results in an empowerment of the lover. The one who in her youth is wholly submissive to Love, and who is strong in virtue, ends up receiving in full freedom "Love's unheard-of power." This power in turn allows the lover to "subdue Love/And be her lord and master" (6.4). In another place she says, "For I understand from the nobility of my soul/That in suffering for sublime Love, I conquer./I will therefore gladly surrender myself/In pain, in repose, in dying, in living" (22.2). For Hadewijch, the most desirable experience is to be reduced to nothingness in Love. But she goes on to say,

> And if anyone then dares to fight Love with
>   longing,
> Wholly without heart and without mind,
> And Love counters this longing with her
>   longing:
> That is the force by which we conquer Love.

The lover must also seek Love in gladness and be willing to brave any obstacle, even death, if she wishes to receive Love. When Love commands, one must be ready to act boldly and be ready to carry out Love's wishes (28.2; 39.4).

Hadewijch follows in the footsteps of Hildegard in her emphasis on a life of virtue. Along with the freedom to choose the good, virtue is the most visible fruit of a love affair with God. The specific virtues of courtly love play a major role in Hadewijch's description of the spiritual life. Fidelity figures in a central role. Love is characterized by unwavering fidelity and Hadewijch is repeatedly counseling the soul to remain faithful to Love—no matter how difficult and painful the slings and arrows of love. In the courtly tradition, a knight's fidelity to his mistress was a supreme value for which any hardship was endured. Given this context, the sacredness of Love's pledge was inviolate and could be utterly trusted (9.3). However, the soul's failure to be faithful was a serious betrayal of the love relationship (22.9).

Hadewijch also relies on the courtly tradition to speak of a second quality of the transformed lover— that of service. The function of a knight toward his lady was one of undying service. He was to be ever ready to respond to the call and the needs of his mistress. For Hadewijch, the call to serve Love is the whole point of being involved with God. As a result of the commitment to serve Love, many hardships ensue (18.2), but this is not to dissuade the soul from the tireless performance of good works.

Good works are not an aspect of the early stages of love that can be left behind as one progresses more deeply into love. On the contrary, Hadewijch counsels: "He who begins to make progress/Must see that he does not lose/Zeal for good works" (6.2). The performance of good works in the early stages of love gives the lover power and immense profit. As a result, she is able to perform all works "with no sign of effort." Fidelity and passionate commitment to Love have results that defy the imagination. The soul is able to live and suffer with little effort or pain (8.3). This way of living is a fruit of love, a sign of a new self in which the earlier experiences have been accepted, embraced and incorporated into one's total existence. The new self is not turned in on itself, but gracefully faces out toward the neighbor and her/his needs.

He who wishes to become Love performs
    excellent works,
For nothing can make him give way;
He is unconquered, and equal in strength
To the task of winning the love of Love,
Whether he serves the sick or the well,
The blind, the crippled or the wounded—
He will accept this as his debt to Love.

To serve strangers, to give to the poor,
To comfort the sorrowful as best he can,
To live in the faithful service of God's friends—
Saints or men on earth—night and day,
With all his might, beyond possibility—
If he thinks his strength will fail,
Let him trust henceforth in reliance on Love
    (8.4, 5).

For all of her talk of the nuances and contours of passionate love, the bottom line for Hadewijch is faithful service to others. She says that some people think they are successful in love because "Mountain and valley burst into bloom." But if one would have the truth, there is little of substance in this sentiment. "By works of fidelity it is fully proved/Whether we gain anything in love" (13.5).

Joy and Optimism

Hadewijch's experience of Love is riddled with enigma and difficulty. Love buffets her with consolation and ill treatment at the same time (31.4). Her whole being cries out to devote herself to noble thoughts of Love, for Love enlarges her heart, luring her to give herself over to Love completely. But if Hadewijch decides to take any free delights or some brief repose in Love's grace, Love storms at her with new commands, deals blows and casts her into prison—even if in a wonderful way (31.1, 2). Yet in the midst of this paradox and confusion, Hadewijch maintains a joy, trust, and openness to Love that is difficult to fathom.

For Hadewijch, Love's ways are ineffable—beyond the ken of the human mind (31.3, 7). But for her, this is no reason to give up or to become cynical. She simply becomes more motivated to continue on her path of fidelity to Love. She has been captivated by the intense experience of Love and she permits nothing to stand in its way. Her text exudes hope and optimism.

Through Love I can fully conquer
My misery and exile;
I know victory will be mine (16.4).

She counsels her readers to be joyful in all seasons
because of Love (30.1). She encourages and exhorts
her sisters not to let their grief distress them. "You
shall soon blossom," she says, "You shall row through
all storms,/Until Beloved and loved one shall wholly
flow through each other" (4.8). The experience of intimacy with the Beloved is worth any price and its con-
summation has been promised by a faithful lover. The
source of her optimism is Love's promise which can be
trusted, her own experience of Love, and Love's inability to withdraw. She says that the soul is to

. . . live in high hope
Of what his heart has chosen.
Love will indeed strengthen him:
He shall conquer his Beloved;
For Love can never
Refuse herself to anyone;
Rather she gives him what she is willing he
      possess,
And more than she herself promised him (6.2).

No matter what happens in the course of the love
affair, the outcome, Hadewijch says, is always joy
(6.3).

From this brief excursus into the world of Hadewijch of Antwerp, we can conclude that she is deeply
immersed and locked into a mutually passionate love
affair with Love. There are other things we could

70

have discussed with profit: her nuanced discussion of the madness of love; her anthropology; the way in which she poetically weaves together a tapestry of opposites; her surprising confidence and self-assurance in the truth of what she has experienced. We have focused on the signs of passion in her description of Love, and the search has not been in vain.

But the love of which Hadewijch speaks does not belong to her alone. It is clear that a primary reason for writing is her desire that others know and enjoy in their own way what she has experienced. Her words reach out from the page, inviting and challenging the reader to follow in her footsteps. She humbly and honestly describes her own experience:

> To be reduced to nothingness in Love
> Is the most desirable thing I know
> Among all the works I have experience of,
> Although I know it is beyond my reach.

And she cries out to others,

> O soul, creature
> And noble image,
> Risk the adventure!
> Consider your law and your nature—
> Which must always love—
> And love the best good of Love.
> To have fruition of her, defend yourself boldly;
> Thus you will have success.
> And spare no hour,
> But ever keep on to the end
> In love (36.6).

CONCLUSION

What may we conclude from this brief exploration into the nature of passionate love as it manifested itself in the religious experience of Hildegard and Hadewijch? To begin, it gives us a view of the function of passion in religious experience in the freshness of its expression. Affective piety of this type had its beginnings in the late eleventh century. One thinks of Augustine as an early precursor, but only in the Middle Ages did large numbers of mystics employ the emotions in a conscious way to move believers toward God. Many mystics expressed this emotion in the form of a personal, passionate attachment to the human Jesus, in a felt connection with the joys and sorrows of the events of his life.[100] The reader is struck by the freedom and spontaneity of expression in this literature. The fear and paranoia that characterize later attitudes toward erotic imagery are notably absent, especially in Hadewijch.

Second, we encounter head-on the Neoplatonic context for this literature. Matter, the world and the body are enemies of the spiritual life. While sexual imagery is used extensively to describe the love affair with God, one is never in doubt about the *spiritual* nature of such imagery and the distance that is always imposed between this experience and human, physical sexuality.

It is not surprising that love among humans was used to help explain love of God, but we no longer pit one against the other. We understand that one does not need to eliminate human loves in order to make room for love of God. Bernard of Clairvaux captures this either/or mentality with a rather brutal image when he speaks about the effect of divine love on human love. "Sweetness conquers sweetness as one nail drives out another."[101]

Today we are aware of the need to discover *connections* between the passionate attachments in our lives and our religious experience. They have the potential to be mutually enhancing. With Rosemary Haughton, I hold that the human sexual relationship is the paradigm or "type" of passion.[102] In its authentic forms (i.e., not driven primarily by selfishness), this relationship involves a drive to know the other, a drive that extends and stretches out to embrace the whole of living and of God. By its very nature, the sexual relationship contains the conditions for its own development toward wholeness. It is time for us as a community to look toward sexuality as an important locus and model for our spiritual lives.

The task of self-reflection lies continually before us. The reasons for shutting out passion are legion. Fear and cowardice close doors to intensity and commitment. It *is* dangerous to live passionately, and some may mistake fanaticism for true passion and be rightly repulsed by it. But the price of such refusal is high. It can cost us our lives, condemning us to pseudo-living and mediocrity.

Third, in our theology, we look to the incarnation as an important foundation for a more wholistic outlook. Christians of every stripe struggle to embrace more fully the ramifications of the incarnation. If all of reality has been definitively made holy by God's taking on flesh in Jesus, then nothing in human life, *a priori,* need be excluded from the sacred. The experience of passion is no exception. There is no reason *not* to look for and find God in the passionate dimensions of our existence—wherever that passion expresses itself. We are also more aware of the passionate expressions and activities of Jesus himself. Who more than he opened himself to others, allowed himself to be led into the fullness of life beyond the law and convention, and suffered the inevitable consequences of this choice? The gospel demand for radical commitment is the same demand that passion makes in its various forms.[103]

One must also note that particularly in Hadewijch's *Poems in Stanzas,* her conception of Love can be used to reach out beyond the confines of the Christian community. In this poetry, Hadewijch does not speak of Love primarily in terms of Jesus or the Christian myth (even though that was clearly the context for her), but in more general, universal terms—terms that are open and potentially helpful to anyone interested in an intense love relationship with the divine.

But Hildegard and Hadewijch are models in a distinctive way for the Christian community. Their willingness to become passionately involved with Christ made them alive with love. They are not boring. Their lives teem with intense participation in life. They said yes to being in love, to the dangers and tribulations of that state as well as to its joys and satisfactions. They lived courageously and allowed love to assist them in the practice of virtues. Letting go to passion made of them different people. At each stage of development another level of newness broke in upon them, leading them to maturity and integrity of life in imitation of their Lover who chose to lay down his life for those whom he loved.

We have come full circle and return to the questions posed at the beginning. In response, we may say that it is indeed possible to broaden the horizons of our understanding of passion. It is possible to allow this new understanding to calm our illegitimate fears and to enhance our wise caution about passion. The refusal of authentic passion produces a life that is flat, indifferent, lukewarm. The women we have studied challenge us to become fully alive, passionate toward God and passionate about becoming saints. They also serve as catalysts nudging us to discover new connections with other forms of passion in life—connections unavailable to them in their age.

Hildegard and Hadewijch stand as reminders that we are not alone in our choice to live and love with passion. They knew intimately a passionate God who freely and generously invited them to share in that passion. They responded affirmatively and call us to do the same. The passion of God is guaranteed to call us out from the moral security of obedience to the law toward our own deepest humanity.[104] Passion involves a transformation in which service to others, healing, relief, comfort, hope and forgiveness take on a radically new character. The person who has allowed passion to have its way returns to love and life and service with new verve and feeling. The experience of passion wounds with the fire of love and opens the door to the utter fullness of humanity in God.

NOTES

1. Mary Warnock, "Religious Imagination," in *Religious Imagination*, ed. James P. Mackey (Edinburgh: Edinburgh University Press, 1986), p. 142.
2. Contemporary western interest in the recovery of affectivity is widespread, e.g., Bernard Lonergan analyzes feelings as the cause of our response to value, and Karl Rahner speaks of ultimate happiness as acceptance of mystery in love. Further, many authors identify the women's movement as an important force behind this recent interest in affectivity. Recovery of the place and dignity of woman has meant the recovery of body and feeling with which she has been culturally identified.
3. W. Gaylin and E. Person, eds. *Passionate Attachments: Thinking About Love* (New York: The Free Press, 1988), pp. ix–xii.
4. Ibid., p. vii.
5. Exceptions include the *Oxford English Dictionary* and the *Dictionnaire de Spiritualité* which devotes eighteen columns to the subject under the heading, "Passions et vie spirituelle."
6. Plotinus, *Enneads* I.8.
7. A. H. Armstrong, "The Ancient and Continuing Pieties of the Greek World," in *Classical Mediterranean Spirituality*, ed. A. H. Armstrong, World Spirituality Series, v. 15. (New York: Crossroad, 1986), p. 70.

8. Armstrong, ibid., p. 85.

9. Ibid.

10. Ibid.

11. Ibid., p. 86. Stoic philosophers included the love of wisdom, as well as feeling and emotion in their concept of reason. They distinguished between good desires and feelings that were part of reason, and passions and mental perturbations that were present in a soul whose reasoning faculty was disordered. In the *City of God* (14.8) Augustine explains this teaching of the Stoics on passion in light of the Christian gospel.

12. This turbulent aspect of love is referred to in Plato's *Symposium* and especially in the *Phaedrus*.

13. See James Conlon, "The Place of Passion: Reflections on 'Fatal Attraction,' " Unpublished paper; and Irving Singer, *The Nature of Love* Vol. 1, *Plato to Luther* (Chicago: University of Chicago Press, 1966), pp. 61–64.

14. Thomas Aquinas offers a dissenting opinion by claiming that passion, while neutral in itself, could by its presence enhance a virtuous act. *Summa theologiae* (Ia IIae, 24.1).

15. See the *Oxford English Dictionary*, s.v. "Passion."

16. Rosemary Haughton, *On Trying To Be Human* (Springfield, IL: Templegate, 1966), pp. 93, 104, 108.

17. Milton Viederman citing student dissertation by Michels. See "The Nature of Passionate Love," in *Passionate Attachments*, p. 4.

18. Milton Viederman distinguishes between passionate and affectionate love. Passionate love occurs in the early stages of a love relationship and is followed by a less intense affectionate love. Viederman also cites Otto Kernberg who chooses to maintain the term passion in both cases, distinguishing between passion as an early stage of a love relationship and passion as the cement

of a more enduring one. See "The Nature of Passionate Love," in *Passionate Attachments,* pp. 1–4.

19. See Irving Singer, *The Nature of Love,* v. 2, p. 32.

20. Rosemary Haughton, *The Passionate God* (New York: Paulist Press, 1981; *On Trying To Be Human* (Springfield, IL: Templegate, 1966).

21. Haughton, *On Trying To Be Human,* p. 93.

22. Ibid., p. 106.

23. Ibid., p. 9.

24. Ibid., p. 18.

25. Ibid., p. 21.

26. Ibid., p. 27.

27. Ibid., p. 26.

28. Ibid., p. 7.

29. Ibid., p. 6.

30. Ibid.

31. Viederman lists as enemies of passion: total understanding of the other, familiarity, certainty, predictability, absolute trust in the other, the disarming of jealousy and legitimization of the relationship. "The Nature of Passionate Love" in *Passionate Attachments,* p. 6. This list suggests a legitimate but limited understanding of passion. In fact, elements of this kind of passion are inimicable to mystical experience inasmuch as the passion of mysticism is predicated on trust in God and a definite kind of legitimacy. However, some of the "enemies" listed by Viederman are reflected in accounts of mystical passion, e.g., God's jealousy, lack of total understanding of God by the mystic, a certain lack of familiarity since the partner in the relationship is ultimate Mystery, etc.

32. William E. Phipps, "The Plight of the Song of Songs," *Journal of the American Academy of Religion* 42 (March 1974): 82.

33. See T.J. Miik, "Babylonian Parallels to the Song of

Songs," *Journal of Biblical Literature* 43 (1924): 245–252; and Michael V. Fox, *The Song of Songs and the Ancient Egyptian Love Songs* (Madison, WI: University of Wisconsin Press, 1985).

34. Marvin H. Pope, trans., *Song of Songs*. Anchor Bible, (New York: Doubleday, 1977), opts for a highly erotic interpretaion. Other scholars such as W. Rudolph and E. Wurthwein opt for a moral interpretation.

35. Origen, *Commentary on the Song of Songs,* 1.4.

36. Sermon 61 in *On the Song of Songs* (Spencer, MA: Cistercian Publications, 1971).

37. *On the Song of Songs,* 20.4.

38. This is also true of recent ecclesiology. See Peter Fransen, *Divine Grace and Man* (New York: The New American Library, 1962), pp. 118-121 and H. Rondet, *The Grace of Christ* (Westminster, MD: Newman Press, 1967), p. 55.

39. Phipps, "The Plight," p. 82.

40. Catalogues in monastic libraries attest to the popularity of the Song. In the twelfth century the library at Cluny listed fifteen commentaries, including those of Origen and Gregory. Among some seventy manuscripts preserved at Orval, there are seven commentaries on the Song. See Jean Leclercq, *The Love of Learning and the Desire for God* (New York: Fordham University Press, 1961), p. 106. In all, there is evidence for some thirty commentaries written during the twelfth century. Some of the more famous Christian commentators on the Song include Origen (d. 254), Gregory of Nyssa (fourth century), Gregory the Great (d. 604), Bede (d. 735), Bernard of Clairvaux (d. 1153), Anselm of Laon (d. 1117) and William of St. Thierry (d. 1148).

41. Beryl Smalley, *Medieval Exegesis of Wisdom Literature* (Atlanta, GA: Scholars Press, 1986), p. 40.

42. Ibid., pp. 107–108.

43. W. Phipps, "The Plight," p. 100.

44. Roland Murphy, "Patristic and Medieval Exegesis—Help or Hindrance?" *The Catholic Biblical Quarterly* 43 (October 1981): 515–516.

45. The constraints of space prohibit examination of other important aspects of passion but we note the importance of the medieval courtly tradition and later romanticism in this regard. See Irving Singer, *The Nature of Love*.

    Passion can also be discussed from other perspectives. For example, the mystical experience is always spoken of as being passive, as something that happens to an individual. However, the passive nature of mysticism should not be understood as lifeless or apathetic. The mystics also note their activity in cooperating with the gift of union with God. One could also study the various intimate connections Christian mystics make between their experience and the passion of Jesus. Although we will not examine these issues in a direct way, it is important to keep them in mind as part of the total context of our subject.

46. This is an argument used by William James in his classic work on mysticism, *Varieties of Religious Experience* (New York: New American Library, 1958).

47. See Cornelius Ernst, *Theology of Grace* (Notre Dame, IN: Fides, 1974), p. 49.

48. Carolyn Walker Bynum, *Jesus as Mother* (Berkeley: University of California Press, 1982), p. 172. Bynum also notes that in gnosticism there was a tradition of seeing the conquest of the passions as a process in which the female became a male. See p. 139, note 98.

49. This focus does not imply that women from other periods do not have mystical experience. One can make a

case for the existence of mystical experience in the early martyrs, such as Perpetua and Felicitas. See Elizabeth A. Petroff, *Medieval Women's Visionary Literature* (New York: Oxford University Press, 1986). We also know that there were desert mothers in the second to fourth centuries, although written evidence is scarce. In the modern period we can point to women such as Evelyn Underhill (d. 1941), Etty Hillesum (d. 1943), Raissa Maritain (d. 1960), and Bernadette Roberts (b. 1931)—women who have had an intense interest in mysticism and/or have recorded their own personal mystical experiences. See Evelyn Underhill, *Mysticism* (New York: E. P. Dutton & Co. 1911); Etty Hillesum, *An Interrupted Life* (New York: Simon & Schuster, 1985); Raissa Maritain, *Raissa's Journal* (Albany, New York: Magi Books, Inc., 1963); Bernadette Roberts, *The Experience of No-Self* (Boston: Shambhala, 1984), and *The Path to No-Self* (Boston: Shambhala, 1985).

50. The historian Henry Osborne Taylor, contrasting classical and medieval sensibilities in 1902, claimed that medieval Christianity attained "heights and depths of emotion undreamed of by antiquity." Cited in T. J. Jackson Lears, *No Place of Grace: Antimodernism and the Transformation of American Culture, 1880–1920* (New York: Pantheon Books, 1981), p. 161.

51. See Bynum, *Jesus as Mother,* pp. 170–172.

52. One must distinguish between accounts of mystical experience written by the women themselves and those written by males, who tended to romanticize and sentimentalize female virtue especially by describing it in heightened and erotic imagery. "If we wish to understand what it meant to medieval women to be 'brides of Christ' . . . we must pay particular attention to what women said and did, avoiding the assumption that

they simply internalized the rhetoric of theologians, confessors, or husbands." Carolyn Bynum, "Religious Women in the Later Middle Ages," in *World Spirituality,* ed. Ewert Cousins, Vol. 17 (New York: Crossroad, 1987), p. 136.

In this essay, we have chosen texts that are quite certainly from the pens of the women themselves or from scribes or eyewitnesses who recorded the words with the intention to write accurately.

53. To supplement this material, one needs to consult more detailed and nuanced monographs on specific women and movements during the medieval period, e.g., Valerie M. Lagorio, "The Medieval Continental Women Mystics: An Introduction" in *An Introduction to the Medieval Mystics of Europe,* ed. Paul E. Szarmach (Albany, NY: SUNY Press, 1984), pp. 161–194.

54. In one of her visions, Hildegard speaks of hearing music: "Therefore, you who are so poor and frail of nature, listen to the sound in this music of the fiery love coming forth in the words of this virginal youth who flowers like a green twig." In *Scivias* (III.13.12).

55. See Barbara Newman, *Sister of Wisdom: St. Hildegard's Theology of the Feminine* (Berkeley: University of California Press, 1987), pp. 10-11. Since Newman examines Hildegard as prophet of wisdom in great detail, we will not include this aspect of Hildegard's thought here. Hildegard does employ erotic imagery when speaking of wisdom: "She [wisdom] has been joined in God and to God in the sweetest embrace in a religious dance of burning love" (*Scivias,* III.9.25).

56. Ibid., p. 65. Hildegard says that the Song of Songs is about those who follow the Word, springing forth green and fruitful with the virtues. The Word, sweet and soft, brings forth holiness and justice (*Scivias* II.6.28).

57. Ibid., p. 15.

58. Kent Kraft, "The German Visionary: Hildegard of Bingen," in *Medieval Women Writers,* ed. Katharina M. Wilson (Athens, GA: University of Georgia Press, 1984), p. 115.

59. This involvement is aided significantly if one is able to view the artistic rendering of the visions in color.

60. All citations are from *Scivias,* trans. Bruce Hozeski (Santa Fe, NM: Bear & Company, 1986). References in the text are to part, vision and section.

61. Letter 9. Fox, p. 292.

62. The use of marriage imagery to describe mystical experiences (known in German as "brautmystik") increased in the twelfth and thirteenth centuries. Carolyn Walker Bynum offers two reasons. The first is the new emphasis on marriage as a sacrament in twelfth century theology and canon law. Second, many spiritual writers of this period entered the monastery later in life. The new monastic orders preferred to recruit adults so that "the percentage of monks and nuns who had been married before their conversion appears to have become much higher." Therefore the experiences of falling in love, courtship and marriage would have been known first-hand. *Jesus as Mother,* p. 142. Hildegard uses daughter imagery as frequently as she uses imagery of the spouse.

63. Although the more powerful impression from Hildegard's text is that of struggle, she does not neglect the element of joy in the life of virtue. In one vision she sees the apostles, martyrs, confessors, virgins and other holy ones walking around with great joy. "The other chosen ones were made to rejoice in the fountain of joy and salvation as the Holy Spirit filled them so that they were flaming and flowing from virtue into virtue" (Ps 84.8) (III.4.11).

64. Barbara Newman, *Sister of Wisdom,* p. 21. Hildegard protests that Mary was never touched by sexual desire (II.6.14). Physical sex pollutes (II.6.26). She offers a minimal endorsement of marriage for procreation alone (III.10.3).

65. Letter 36. In *Hildegard of Bingen's Book of Divine Works with Letters and Songs,* ed. Matthew Fox (Santa Fe, NM: Bear & Co. 1987), p. 344.

66. Letter 40. Fox, p. 352.

67. Occasionally Hildegard uses the image of blood, by means of which the Holy Spirit surrounds and warms humans. In other texts, blood symbolizes defilement and slavery to burning fleshly desires (III.7.8). For an extended treatment of the function of blood symbolism for many medieval women mystics, see Carolyn Bynum, *Jesus as Mother,* pp. 131, 151f.

68. Hildegard's obvious passion for acting justly and for calling others to do likewise does not obliterate the passive dimension of the mystical experience, of being a mere vehicle for *God's* activity. In a letter to Elisabeth of Schönau, a younger contemporary of Hildegard's and a mystic, she says that visionaries and prophets, knowing nothing of heavenly things, "only sing forth God's secrets, like a trumpet that merely gives out sounds, and does not itself labor, but another blows into it, so that it might yield a sound." She compares her own utterances to "the weak sound of a trumpet from the living light" (Letter 34. Fox, p. 340). Margaret Wade Labarge uses this trumpet image for the title of her book, *A Small Sound of the Trumpet: Women in Medieval Life* (Boston: Beacon Press, 1986).

69. One scholar sees in this conflict evidence of the perennial struggle between charism and institution in the church. See A. Fuhrkotter, *Briefsechsel: Nach den altesten*

Handschriften ubersetzt und nach den Quellen erlautert, pp. 235–246.

70. Newman, *Sister of Wisdom,* p. 9.
71. Scholars have investigated the physical causes of visionary and hallucinatory experience. Charles Singer attributes the visions to migrainous "scintillating scotoma." See "The Scientific Views and Visions of Saint Hildegard" in *Studies in the History and Method of Science,* pp. 1–55. Discussed in Kraft, "The German Visionary," p. 119.
72. Letter 39. Fox, p. 350.
73. Hildegard also presents a God who is impatient with the poor who waste what is given to them out of greed (II.6.91).
74. Haughton, *On Trying To Be Human,* p. 137.
75. Letter 26. Fox, p. 331.
76. See Newman, *Sister of Wisdom,* pp. 137–138.
77. *Die Echtheir des Schrifttums der heiligen Hildegard von Bingen: Quellenkritische Untersuchungen,* ed. Marianna Schrader and Adelgundis Fuhrkotter, p. 137. Cited in Kraft, "The German Visionary," in *Medieval Women Writers,* p. 111.
78. Kraft, "The German Visionary," in *Medieval Women Writers,* p. 112.
79. Hadewijch is variously placed in Antwerp or Brussels. The dialect in which she wrote is Brabant. The main source for all Hadewijch scholarship is Jos van Mierlo who has edited her entire corpus, 1924–1952.
80. Mother Columba Hart, Introduction, *Hadewijch: The Complete Works* (New York: Paulist Press, 1980), p. 1.
81. Ibid., Preface, p. xiii.
82. Other important beguines include Marie of Oignies, one of the earliest beguines, Mechtild of Magdeburg, a well known thirteenth century mystic, and Marguerite

of Porete, whose impassioned criticism of the weak-
nesses in the church led to her being accused of heresy
and burnt at the stake in Paris in 1310. Beguine communities at Bruges, Louvain, Lier and Diest survive to this
day, witnessing to the continuing relevance of the
beguine lifestyle.

83. Margaret Wade Labarge, *A Small Sound of the Trumpet*,
p. 115.

84. Ibid.

85. Hart, *Hadewijch*, Introduction, pp. 4–5.

86. Ria Vanderauwera, "The Brabant Mystic: Hadewijch,"
in *Medieval Women Writers*, p. 186. Hadewijch uses several different terms for "love." "Karitate" usually refers
to love of neighbor; "lief" refers to the beloved who is
either Christ or the soul; "minne," a word of feminine
gender and belonging to the language of courtly love,
is used most often. See Hart, *Hadewijch*, Introduction,
p. 8.

87. Ibid., p. 188. Vanderauwera refers here to the work of N.
de Paepe, *Hadewijch: Strofische Gedichten* (Ghent, 1967).

88. Cited in Vanderauwera, p. 188.

89. Tanis Guest shows how Hadewijch made use of the
conventions of the courtly love song: nature opening,
tripartition, tornada, rhyme scheme, concatenation,
and imagery. *Some Aspects of Hadewijch's Poetic Form in
the "Strofische Gedichten"* (The Hague, 1975). Cited in
Vanderauwera, p. 189.

90. Vanderauwera, p. 189.

91. Hart, *Hadewijch*, Introduction, p. 19.

92. Vanderauwera, p. 188. At the end of the thirteenth
century there was a vigorous reaction against courtly
poetry and it is supposed that much of it has been lost.
Vanderauwera suggests that Hadewijch's poetry sur-
vived because of its religious, i.e., "safe" content.

93. See Paul Mommaers, "Hadewijch: A Feminist in Conflict," *Louvain Studies* 13 (1988), p. 69. In Letter 30, Hadewijch relates the life of love to the Trinity. Reason, motivating one to perfection, reflects the Son; the will of Love that leads one to exercise the virtues ardently belongs to the Spirit; the drive to imitate God in every way is connected to the Father.

94. References in the text are to the poem and stanza number in *Hadewijch: The Complete Works,* ed. Mother Columba Hart.

95. Mommaers, "Hadewijch: A Feminist in Conflict," pp. 64–65.

96. Hart, *Hadewijch,* Introduction, pp. 11–12.

97. Mommaers, "Hadewijch: A Feminist in Conflict," p. 65. Focus on the humanity of Jesus is *not* a focus in the *Poems in Stanzas.* Therefore we look to her *Letters* and *Visions* for the material in this section.

98. Trans. Mother Columba Hart, in *Medieval Women's Visionary Literature,* ed. Elizabeth Alvilda Petroff (New York: Oxford University Press, 1986), p. 195.

99. Haughton, *On Trying To Be Human,* pp. 98–99.

100. See Clarissa Atkinson, *Mystic and Pilgrim: The "Book" and the World of Margery Kempe* (Ithaca, NY: Cornell University Press, 1983), p. 129.

101. Bernard of Clairvaux, *On the Song of Songs,* 2.150.

102. *On Trying To Be Human,* p. 106.

103. Ibid., p. 110.

104. Haughton sees adherence to the law as a crucial preparation, enabling one to discern the authentic demand of passion from the fantasies of escapism and self-indulgence. But the law is not enough in itself to satisfy the need of the human spirit for the fullness of self-discovery. *On Trying To Be Human,* p. 110.

Elizabeth A. Dreyer, Ph.D., is assistant professor in the Department of Ecclesiastical History at the Washington Theological Union in Silver Spring, Md. She is the author of numerous articles on the history of spirituality, and of a forthcoming book, *Manifestations of Grace*. She is married to John Bennett, Ph.d. They reside in Adrian, Mich.